SURVIVING
A Personal Guide to Judicia
in Ireland

About the author

Surviving is Anne McLoughlin's first book. Having been through a judicial separation herself, she was motivated to write her own easy-to-understand guide to help others through the process. She is currently working on her next project.

Anne is now divorced and lives happily in Dublin with her young daughter.

SURVIVING

*A Personal Guide to Judicial
Separation in Ireland*

Anne McLoughlin

TOWN
HOUSE
DUBLIN

First published in 2004 by
TownHouse, Dublin
THCH Ltd
Trinity House
Charleston Road
Ranelagh
Dublin 6
Ireland

www.townhouse.ie

© Anne McLoughlin, 2004

1   2   3   4   5   6   7   8   9   10

All rights reserved. No part of this publication may be reproduced,
stored in a retrieval system, or transmitted in any form or by any
means, electronic, mechanical, photocopying, recording or
otherwise, without the prior permission of the publisher.
A CIP catalogue record for this book is available from the British
Library.

© pp 187–193, The Legal Aid Board, reproduced by permission.

© pp 117–120, 125–130, 179–182,
The Department of Justice, reproduced by permission.

ISBN: 1–86059–229–5

Typeset by Red Barn Publishing, Skeagh, Skibbereen
Printed by Creative Print & Design (Wales) Ltd, Ebbw Vale

CONTENTS

Acknowledgements   vii

Introduction   ix

1   Types of separation   1

2   The right solicitor for you   12

3   Barristers   30

4   Representing yourself – acting lay litigant   44

5   Legal aid   60

6   How the courts work   73

7   What the courts can make judgments on   90

8   Other lessons I learned about the courts   108

9   Working out your finances   114

10   The maintenance myth   134

11   Access   147

12   Pre-nuptial agreements   155

13   Paperwork   159

14   Looking ahead   180

Appendix   187

Index   193

To Mum and Dad.
Thank you for all your constant love and
support.

ACKNOWLEDGEMENTS

There are so many people I would like to thank, they would fill a book of their own. Firstly, I would like to thank all my family, in particular Mum and Dad, for everything – it is much appreciated. Nuala, for just being you and being so truly wonderful; don't ever change, you are one of life's angels.

For my beautiful daughter Hannah, who colourfully crayoned many drafts of this book and who lights up every day with her laughter – my wonderful bundle of joy.

To Ken Deale of Kenneth Deale and Associates, not only for his assistance with this book but for being the kind of solicitor I needed in my time of crisis – thank you for your kindness and professionalism.

Naomi, Anita and Dee – despite my often distracted ways, your gift of friendship both individually and collectively is one of the things most precious to me – thank you for everything, my life is richer because of each of you. Orflaith, for so many moments, most of which make me heartily laugh.

Niall and Rory, two of life's gentlemen, for that fateful day – never forgotten – I am forever in your debt. Stephanie and Brendan, for your much-loved open house and safe haven. Keith and Maria – truly wonderful people. Carole, founder member of the gals, and Emer and Kyrle for being exactly what a girl needs nearby. Alan, for your friendship and support.

For all my friends – Caron (so many laughs), Liz, Jenny, Rachel, Aedin, Mayo and all of you – you know who you are – thank you.

I would like to gratefully acknowledge the help and advice of Dara Mullally and Michelle O'Mahony of the

Legal Aid Board, Elaine Nolan of the Government Publications Office, and Liam Edwards of the MABS Unit, Department of Social and Family Affairs.

To Treasa, Helen, Aislinn and Deirdre and the truly wonderful team at TownHouse – for the way they handled this publication and for taking a chance on me.

INTRODUCTION

A thought strikes me as I write the final cheque to my solicitors for fees in excess of €30,000 – I would never have spent that much in a million years (and indeed didn't) on my wedding and honeymoon combined. Nor did I envisage, when I took my wedding vows, that 'until death do us part' would turn into 'until legal separation do us part'.

For most people, a wedding day is a time of promise and optimism. I believed that I would spend the rest of my days with the same person, sharing everything that crossed our paths, building a future together, maybe one day even having children. For me, marriage was a commitment for life, and the thought of separation or divorce did not enter my head. Separation was something that happened to other people in some parallel universe, but it would never touch my life. Less than eighteen months later, it did.

The feelings evoked by the end of a marriage are different for everyone. Usually, one of the earliest feelings is a sense of total and utter isolation, so let me put that one to bed right away. If you are reading this because you are facing the end of your marriage, let me welcome you to a large and rather inclusive group, a group that is not open to just a select few but that is growing all the time, a group which you only really become aware of when you join. It has no gender bias, social barriers or qualifications for joining and its members range across all age groups, social circles and walks of life.

I have now journeyed from one end of the separation process to the other and survived. As with marriage, lessons are learned by making mistakes along the way. However, such mistakes can be costly, both financially and emotionally. The obvious course would be to learn from others who have trodden that path before. Unfortunately, at the time my journey started there was a severe lack of reading material available to help me on my way and give me the benefit of others' experience. I am not talking about legal reference books written by the service providers – solicitors, barristers and judges – but about books written by people who have been through the process and reported it from the viewpoint of the separated person. This has prompted me to share my experience of the pitfalls I encountered and lessons I learned along the way, which will hopefully make your journey smoother and less costly, both emotionally and financially.

I am not a solicitor or a barrister; I am a consumer of the services provided by such professionals. I believe that the information I have assembled here, drawn from my own experiences of the separation process, will provide an essential starting-point and reference for others facing the same situation. Trying to absorb and remember a large amount of complex information is difficult, and it can be hard to stay objective when applying it to your own set of circumstances. This book describes both the information I was provided with and the practical application I found it to have, as well as my own personal experiences. It is not legal advice, nor is it meant to replace professional legal advice, which should always be sought, but it aims to give the perspective and advice of a survivor of the judicial separation system in Ireland.

On 27 February 1997, divorce was legalised in Ireland. This was the result of a national referendum. It was a close call, as the 'yes' vote barely scraped in, but it did, and for that many people give thanks. I voted 'yes' as a single person, little knowing how grateful I would be that I had taken the time to cast that vote.

For anyone to qualify for divorce, they must have been separated for at least four out of the previous five years. The breakdown of a marriage puts incredible strain, both emotional and financial, on both parties. This can make it impossible and indeed completely impractical to wait four years before addressing issues such as maintenance, property, access and the many other things that enter the arena of division when a marriage ends. When it comes to making decisions about such important issues, both parties need to be feeling alert and capable, instead of which they are often experiencing considerable distress and consequent lethargy, making the decision-making process all the more difficult.

Divorce may be a relatively new concept in Irish society, but the breakdown of a marriage is not. For those who cannot wait the four years before qualifying to make an application for divorce, an alternative solution must be sought. That alternative is a judicial separation.

Finding yourself in a position where one or both partners want a separation can be one of the most challenging experiences a person can go through. Not only will you have to deal with your own feelings, but you will also have to deal with the reactions of family and friends and all the practical issues that tend to surface all too rapidly, particularly when there are children involved. This can be an emotional rollercoaster and you may not have a clue where to start. I know I didn't.

I entered my own separation process with a huge degree of naivety and uncertainty. I had no idea what lay ahead of me. While there are many people and organisations that are more than willing to help, it can be difficult and time-consuming to find out the kind of information you need to know. In the two and a half years it took me to obtain my judicial separation, I learned a lot. I also met some of the most amazing people, many of whom I now have the privilege to count among my friends. Finally, I have survived the judicial separation process as a stronger and wiser person, but some of the mistakes I made along the way not only cost me financially but, more importantly, also cost me in terms of time and energy.

If I had known at the beginning what I know now, my journey would have been shorter, less painful and stressful and a whole lot cheaper. The purpose of writing this book is to help people who find themselves in this situation and to share the information and experiences I have gathered from many different sources. This book will help manage your expectations and provide a road map for your journey. Think of it as your companion, as a practical support throughout the process. I hope it will help you survive separation in Ireland.

Anne McLoughlin
September 2004

[1]

TYPES OF
SEPARATION

In a consumer market, there is always a range of choices. Even milk comes as full fat, low fat or skimmed. So, too, there is some choice when undergoing separation, not about the final outcome of two people separating but about the medium whereby they choose to do it.

When a marriage breaks down and the two partners, to all intents and purposes, are now only married in name, some form of agreement or solution will inevitably need to be reached about the practical day-to-day facts of life: bills, finances, living arrangements, children, etc. Suddenly, costs which were shared are now separate and some are even effectively doubled. Both parties may need to find separate accommodation. Children who have shared a roof and home with both parents as a family unit will now have to come to terms with seeing each parent individually on separate occasions and, for one or both of those parents, in a new environment, potentially with a new partner and family further down the road. Each partner's network of family and friends inevitably changes and so do their lifestyles and living arrangements.

There are a number of ways whereby an acceptable solution can be reached for both parties in achieving a legal separation and subsequent divorce.

When asked 'What should I do?', I always give the same advice: do everything possible not to end up going to court. Court is really the last-chance saloon, the place you turn to when all other possibilities have been exhausted and you really have no other choice. Going to court is an expensive, tiring and emotionally draining process which should only be entered into with careful consideration, and only after exhausting every other option. I cannot stress this strongly enough. No one should have to go to court, so, if you can possibly keep yourself out of court, do so. If that means swallowing your pride and reaching a difficult agreement with your estranged spouse, then swallow your pride. No matter how hurt you are or how much you may want to strike back, court is not the place to do so. The process of going to court is like chaining together two people who often cannot stand the sight of each other until a solution is passed down and they go their separate ways – not a pretty picture. The two people are brought together to have a legal argument with set rules and referees, just like a boxing match. For many it is a necessary evil, as it provides the only way of reaching an agreement and putting a formal solution in place. For some, those set rules and procedures are welcome, because the alternatives are far worse and the courts are their only recourse. However, if it is not absolutely essential, think again.

No legal system in the world is perfect. By their nature, courts often have to make some difficult decisions which may not always be supported by the parties involved. There is always the appeals mechanism, whereby you can challenge the decision handed down by the court, but this inevitably costs more in terms of time, money and energy. However, court is not your only option. Below are various options open to you:

~ Separation agreement
~ Nullity
~ Mediated agreement
~ Legal/judicial separation
~ Divorce

Separation agreement

A separation agreement is where both parties separate and reach their own agreement about how they want to work out all the practical issues. While initially this may seem ridiculous and unrealistic, it is a real option. If the separation agreement breaks down, a more formal solution is usually sought. A separation agreement can work in a number of ways. Agreement can be reached in connection with living arrangements – who, if anyone, remains in the family home – or the division of previously shared assets, everything from the CD collection to the division of major assets. Where there are children, agreement can also be reached about maintenance payments and access arrangements, depending on the age of the children and the circumstances of both parties. For example, if both parties work full time the arrangements for access to children may differ from a situation where one partner is in full-time employment and the other is not.

An arrangement like this can be a private arrangement between two people, with no one else involved and with no formal written agreement – just two people agreeing to live in a different way. Alternatively, the agreement can be agreed between both partners and formalised in writing by a solicitor. If both are in total agreement, two solicitors (each partner should have their own) can be used to draft a separation agreement. There will be no need to go to court to get a court-ordered separation. The solicitors can draw up the agreement and both partners sign it. An agreement produced in this way is valid, even though it does not emanate from the courts. However, it would not have the power to bind pension trustees, whereas a court-ordered agreement would, although you can set out your intentions in the agreement and the trustees can be made aware of them. This is the most financially inexpensive way to reach a legal separation.

Nullity

There are two types of annulment: a state annulment and a church annulment. Both have completely different jurisdictions. A state annulment is applied for through the legal system and a church annulment is applied for through the church. The law of the land applies to the state annulment and canon law, or the law of the church, applies to the latter. Neither one has any bearing or effect on the other.

When a marriage is nullified, this returns both people to their status prior to marrying, as though the marriage had never existed. A state nullity gives both parties the right to remarry in the state under a civil ceremony (registry office), but not the right to remarry within the church.

A church annulment has no effect on the legal status of a marriage. It simply nullifies the marriage in the eyes of the church and may, in effect, allow the two parties to remarry in a church in the eyes of God. However, the parties would have to no longer be married in the eyes of the state as well for this to happen. This means that anyone who is divorced or has a state annulment in

Ireland and a church annulment can remarry, both in the eyes of the state (in a registry office) and in the eyes of the church (a church wedding).

The effect of a nullity is really to say that the marriage never existed. If you feel you have grounds for a nullity, you should seek legal advice in relation to this.

If a state nullity is applied for, you should be aware that, if granted, it does change many things. For example, a family home is only a family home if the couple occupying it are married. If the marriage is state annulled, it may no longer be considered to be the family home and, if one party had bought it prior to the marriage, it may in effect be sold by that person without the other person's consent. It can also affect such things as maintenance, as there is only an obligation to pay maintenance for a spouse if there had been a marriage, and a state nullity would have the effect of saying the marriage had never existed. It does not affect the succession rights of children of the two parties; however, it may bring such things as parental guardianship into the arena. It is not necessarily the case that rights of guardianship are reversed when a marriage is state annulled; a father can often retain his guardianship rights. An application for nullity will not be considered, nor should it be sought, as a way of trying to circumvent financial responsibilities or trying to reduce/remove a partner's financial rights.

Mediated separation agreement

The difference between a mediated agreement and a court decision is that the people who make the decision in a mediated agreement are the two people involved. This is the most important difference between the two and, by its nature, makes it a far less adversarial route to take. In a mediated agreement, the mediator discusses the issues with both parties together. If an agreement is reached, it is formalised in a document called a 'Heads of Agreement', which is signed by both parties. This document is not legally binding but should provide a basis for a formal separation agreement, whereby the document is modified to include any changes desired by either party after taking legal advice from their solicitors. It is obviously cheaper, quicker and less stressful if the separation agreement can be largely agreed beforehand in a Heads of Agreement. While both parties may never speak a word to each other again after the whole process is complete, it would probably increase the chances of a more amicable solution and create less bitterness in the long term from both an emotional and a financial perspective. A judicial separation through the courts can take months and even in some cases years. Mediated agreements can sometimes be finalised after meetings amounting to between two and six hour-long sessions, although this could obviously be more for some couples. No mediated agreement can make provisions that bind pensions. This can only be done by court-ordered separation, which is legally binding.

If you decide to file for a judicial separation, or indeed if judicial proceedings have been initiated by your estranged spouse, your solicitor is required by law to discuss the possibility of mediation as a means of reaching a solution. The solicitor should provide you with a list of names and addresses of individuals and organisations that are qualified to help people reach a mediated agreement; some of these services are free and some have costs attached. The solicitor is legally required to file a document with the courts stating that they have advised you appropriately if you choose to take the legal route.

Stop right there. Listen to what the solicitor has to say and at least take some time to think about it. If you try mediation and it doesn't work, you can just continue down the road of judicial separation. At least then, if you do take the judicial separation route, you will have no doubts about it. The legal process can be very taxing and you need to be sure that you have no alternative.

Judicial separation

If you leave your partner because you no longer like the colour of his/her hair or because you do not like the aftershave/perfume s/he uses, this will not be viewed by the courts as a valid reason for applying for a judicial separation. There are a number of reasons that are acceptable to the courts which you can list when making your application. One of these grounds must exist before the court will proceed with your application.

Some people may view the court as a means of airing their grievances or a way of getting back at a spouse by listing things in the affidavit to cause hurt or pain. Don't do it. No one cares and you will only be wasting your time and energy. It may also have a negative influence on the court's perception of you. I know it is a time when it is hard to remain objective, but find a different way to work through or air those grievances. This is not the appropriate forum.

GROUNDS FOR JUDICIAL SEPARATION

~ One party has committed adultery.

~ One party has behaved in such a way that it would be unreasonable to expect the other spouse to continue to live with them.

~ One party has deserted the other for at least one year at the time of the application.

~ The parties have lived apart from one another for one year up to the time of the application and both parties agree to the decree being granted.

~ The parties have lived apart from one another for at least three years at the time of the application for the decree (whether or not both parties agree to the decree being granted).

~ The court considers that a normal marital relationship has not existed between the spouses for at least one year before the date of the application for the decree.

Grounds for seeking a judicial separation

As you can see, most of the grounds for judicial separation do not involve the courts in deciding who is at fault in the separation.

While Ireland has a 'no fault' policy, the court may choose to take into consideration the behaviour of both or either spouse if it is felt to be relevant to the case.

If one party has a history of violence against the other, or against any children of the marriage, this can have a huge bearing on certain orders, such as access. A court may consider mitigating circumstances, so make sure your solicitor is aware of them. The court will not, however, facilitate two parties who wish to use the court to air grievances and take a swipe at each other. Its prime concern is to move both parties forward, and it is not interested in rehashing the past where it is not relevant.

Divorce

Divorce – the final frontier. Divorce is a formal and final legal separation which leaves both parties free to remarry. This is one of the fundamental differences between judicial separation and divorce. If you are applying for a divorce and have not been through the judicial separation process, all the things that are normally sorted out in that process need to be addressed in the divorce process. A divorce will not be granted unless the court is satisfied that all necessary provisions have been made for both spouses and any children of the marriage.

For many, divorce is just a process of dotting the i's and crossing the t's. If it is an uncontested divorce, particularly where a separation agreement or a judicial separation is already in place and of recent vintage, it can sometimes be a process that takes no more than ten minutes. Both spouses may be asked to give testimony to some specific questions.

- ∾ What was the date of the marriage? (The original copy of the marriage certificate, which the solicitor will require as part of the process, must be confirmed as indeed being the marriage certificate.)
- ∾ How long have both parties been separated? (This must be an aggregate of at least four years out of the last five.)
- ∾ Is there any prospect of reconciliation?
- ∾ Is there proper provision in place for both parties and the children?

The court must be satisfied that the requirements of the legislation and the Constitution are met.

A few other questions may be asked, at the discretion of the court – nothing too taxing. Once these are answered to the satisfaction of the court, the judge will usually grant the divorce and each party will leave the courtroom as a single person.

If divorce is your first stab at forging a legal separation, many more things may come under the hammer, just as in a judicial separation. These issues will have to be decided on before a divorce is granted, so the hearing will take a lot longer than ten minutes.

When a person has a separation agreement or judicial separation, s/he is still legally married. When a person is divorced, s/he is no longer legally married. The terms of a separation agreement or judicial separation can come up for renegotiation at the time of divorce. Some issues in relation to access and maintenance can be revisited at this point; indeed, any issue can be revisited at this point. If, however, certain awards have already been made by the court in regard to a judicial separation, unless there has been a change in circumstances the person may have an uphill struggle in having them addressed again as part of the divorce proceedings. The reason that access and maintenance can come up again is because these orders can tend to change according to changes in circumstances (for example, access may vary as children get older and as their needs change over the ensuing years). The maintenance order is more than likely to change also, as expenses and financial circumstances change over the years.

To apply for a divorce, you must have been separated for at least four out of the five previous years.

In deciding the best type of separation for you, getting good legal advice on the specific circumstances of your case may be helpful.

[2]

THE RIGHT SOLICITOR FOR YOU

A mong the many platitudes you may hear when you first tell people you are newly separated is 'I hope you have a good solicitor', and in truth there is a lot to be said for having a good solicitor. But how do you find one? How do you know if s/he is truly the right solicitor for you? How do you know what you really need and if any given solicitor is going to be able to provide it?

Like many fairy tales, this chapter is something of a cautionary tale. It stems from one memory of sitting in a crowded waiting area in the family court and listening to a solicitor chatting on a mobile between his cases. He was talking to what appeared to be a friend, arranging to meet up at the weekend to look at some paintings that he was considering buying as an investment by a new and upcoming artist (unfortunately, the name of the artist escapes me). As this conversation was drawing to an end, I was struck by the picture of those fellow travellers surrounding me. All seemed very subdued and many were quite visibly tense and nervous. The contrast between these two scenarios has always stayed in my mind. I tell this tale because it confirms one thing: clients may leave a courtroom in a financially worse position than when they went in, but solicitors will not, so bear this in mind before you spend your money.

What solicitors do

So, let us start at the beginning. What is a solicitor and what is the purpose of using one? There are over 5,000 registered firms of solicitors in Ireland, dealing with all aspects of the law. A solicitor's job is to provide a client with up-to-date legal advice relevant to the client's specific situation, to advise clients of all legal remedies, prepare all the legal paperwork for briefing a barrister and appearing in court, deal with all correspondence from the opposing side and ensure that all the paperwork required by a court process is completed. The purpose of retaining a solicitor is to have someone represent the client legally, in this case in dealing with an estranged spouse (which usually occurs through his/her solicitor), and to receive advice on the best course of action, in the knowledge that the solicitor is properly conversant with the full remit of the law.

Whether or not you end up using a solicitor at the end of the day (you are not obliged to), seeking professional advice from an impartial source can never be a bad thing. People who are emotionally involved with you may only tell you what they think you want to hear, which may be substantially removed from reality. Paying an impartial professional should ensure that you receive more realistic and accurate advice. However, although every solicitor will advise you according to the current status of the law, opinions as to the potential outcome of a case may vary slightly – and sometimes greatly – from solicitor to solicitor. Their advice can be subjective, depending on their level of experience and their range of exposure to your type of case.

How to find the best solicitor for you

There are many ways of finding a solicitor. These may include the following:

- ~ by personal recommendation (someone you know may have been through something similar);

- ~ by using a family solicitor who may be known to your family (if unable to help in the area of family law, s/he may be able to advise you on who to use by providing you with a referral);

- ~ through press coverage or word of mouth; or

- ~ by getting out the yellow pages, looking through the ads and trying out a few to find the best fit.

Know your needs – amicable or adversarial separation

Separation for every couple is different. Some couples separate after twenty years of marriage, several children and a lifetime of working together. Others separate after only one or two years, have no children and are both working full time and can financially support themselves. Every case is different. Your needs and what it is you need to achieve in court will influence the kind of legal representation you require.

If things are relatively amicable, in that you have been able to achieve a mediated solution (see Chapter 1) that does not require the involvement of a court, the main job of a solicitor will be to prepare the legal paperwork that is necessary to legalise such a decision. If things are completely hostile and you are unable to communicate on any front with your estranged spouse, you may require a solicitor who is better qualified to guide you through the often-troubled waters of a court battle. I deliberately use the word 'battle', as in most cases the court system is adversarial, with the two parties arguing opposite sides of the same case. It also tends to be adversarial because, by the time the case reaches the court, all alternative avenues have usually been exhausted and an amicable solution has become impossible. In effect, an impartial stranger – the judge – assesses the merits of the case and makes a decision which will be legally binding and can be enforced through further remedies of the court.

No matter what your needs, the best advice is to shop around. If you are making any major purchase in your life, you are most likely to look in more than one place – test-driving more than one car, looking at more than one wedding venue, trying on more than one pair of shoes. So do not be tempted to take the first solicitor on offer just because you are in crisis. The most important work is often in the groundwork. Take the time you need to find the person that is going to suit your needs, your personality and your pocket. There is no point in having a hotshot solicitor who is never available to take your calls and does not listen to what it is you want. At the same time, you do not want someone who promises to 'get you every penny' your spouse has – because that kind of solicitor is often the worst kind.

While needing a solicitor who truly knows his/her stuff, where you are on the emotional yardstick at the time of choosing one may influence your decision quite significantly. Good solicitors are worth their weight in gold. They will – or at least should – ease the pain of the entire process by being both a fountain of legal knowledge and a buffer in your time of crisis. If you are further on along the emotional yardstick and require less of a buffer, this will make the choice of solicitor more straightforward.

How to get the best out of your initial consultation

Most family law solicitors will see you for an initial consultation, when they will establish the facts of your case and advise you as to the best course of action. This does not mean that they are now retained as your solicitor; it is up to you to consider the following questions.

- ∽ Do you feel you can trust this person to deal with your case?

- ∽ Do you feel s/he has given you practical and impartial legal advice, regardless of whether or not you liked what you heard?

- ∽ Do you believe s/he listened to you – really listened to you – and heard your needs?

- ∽ Who spoke most at the meeting? Did the solicitor regale you with tales of previous cases or did s/he spend the time you are paying for asking questions relevant to your case and citing occasional references?

~ Do you believe you can work with this person
to help you achieve the best solution for you?

An initial consultation with a solicitor can cost
anything up to €150 (excluding VAT). This amount
should be deductible from your final bill if you choose to
have him/her represent you. I believe that this is the best
money you will spend in the entire process of acquiring a
separation. A judicial separation through the courts
without legal aid can cost each party anything between
€12,000 and €50,000 (and sometimes even more), so
this initial charge is quite insignificant at the end of the
day and may save you thousands in the long run.

Before you meet with any solicitor, get a pen and a pad
of paper and make some notes. It is amazing what you
can forget. Use this as a shopping list to guide you when
making your decision about which solicitor to choose
and use it with every solicitor you see (yes, you should see
more than one), as this is the easiest way to draw
comparisons. Never meet with a solicitor unless you have
briefly jotted down the points you wish to discuss.
Memory can be a funny thing, particularly if you are
stressed, so note down the answers you get too.

It is also a good idea to at least have some idea of what
you hope to achieve by choosing the legal route before you
make your choice. Hard as it may be, it is important to try
to be realistic about your expectations. Dividing two lives
means dividing financial assets and aspirations, and this is
something you should prepare yourself to deal with.

To sum up, don't be distracted by a solicitor who
promises you everything. Make your decision based on
the facts.

How to manage your solicitor – establishing the facts

There is an expression that says that a solicitor is only as good as his/her client. The information you provide to your solicitor is the foundation on which your case will be based and which will govern the kind of advice you will be given. This information should be assimilated at the first meeting in order to give you and your solicitor a full picture by which to measure the merits of your case.

Below is a list of questions your solicitor may ask in order to establish the facts of your case.

- ~ What was the date of your marriage?
- ~ How long was your courtship prior to marriage?
- ~ Have you any children? If you have, how many are there and how old are they?
- ~ What childcare facilities or schools do your children attend and how much do they cost?
- ~ Have your children any special healthcare, learning or other needs?
- ~ Who are the children living with and does the non-resident partner have access? If so, when and for how long?
- ~ Are you employed? Give details.
- ~ How much do you earn?
- ~ Is your spouse employed? What is his/her job and where? How much does your spouse earn?
- ~ Where do you live and what are your living circumstances? (Are you paying a mortgage, renting or living with other family members?)

~ What are your outgoings in relation to mortgage payments/rent/other loans?

~ How is the mortgage/rent paid and who pays it?

~ Do you have any investments, other property or shares? If you own the family home, is this the only shared asset?

~ Was the family home purchased together? If not, was it bequeathed to one spouse or bought prior to the marriage by one spouse and then shared by the other?

~ If one partner owned the family home prior to marriage, how long did s/he own it prior to you moving in?

~ What was your financial input into the marriage?

~ Are there any assets held solely in the name of one or other spouse?

~ Are you currently paying or receiving maintenance for yourself or for any children of the marriage?

~ Were your children born prior to or subsequent to your marriage?

~ Why did your marriage break down?

~ Is there any chance of reconciliation? Have you tried working things out amicably, either by yourselves or through mediation?

~ What are your financial needs and your monthly outgoings?

~ How amicable do you feel your estranged spouse is likely to be?

~ What do you hope to achieve from a settlement awarded in court?

Based on the above, a solicitor should be able to establish the facts of the case and give you some idea of what he or she believes you can expect. Remember, though, that this may vary from one solicitor to another – it is not an exact science.

Buyer beware

If your reason for seeking a solicitor is to exact revenge on your spouse, then you will be sorely disappointed. No solicitor can promise a guaranteed outcome when going to court. However, a good solicitor will tell you what you should aim to achieve and what they believe is reasonable, nothing more.

Furthermore, if you are looking for a solicitor to help you reduce your financial liability in relation to your estranged spouse, for instance by helping you conceal your financial assets, think again. All solicitors are bound by a strict code of conduct, which does not include encouraging a client to defraud another party or misrepresent oneself in court. A solicitor is an officer of the court and is bound by code of ethics within the legal system. They should not be party to anything which constitutes a misrepresentation of a client's position. So, if you have a million euro stashed away in some bank account, your solicitor cannot assist you in falsifying your true financial position. If you and your spouse, as a couple, have previously used a solicitor for other legal matters, that solicitor should not represent either of you in a family law situation and you can object if they do.

What you should expect from your solicitor

A solicitor will provide you with legal advice throughout the course of your case, according to the specific issues that arise. However, in my opinion a good solicitor should provide you with the following information after an initial consultation:

- ∽ A solicitor is legally obliged to provide you with details of counselling services to assist in a reconciliation. The solicitor is also obliged to furnish you with details of mediation services that can assist both parties in drafting a 'Heads of Agreement' document, which can subsequently be amended after legal advice and provide the foundation for a separation agreement.

- ∽ The solicitor should advise you as to the most relevant court for your case to be heard in (i.e. circuit or high court) and the reasons why it should be heard in such a court. Different courts have the power to make different financial orders, and this is something you should be made aware of.

- ∽ A solicitor should give some indication as to what kind of settlement you should be looking for, and what, in their opinion, you may hope to achieve.

- ∽ A solicitor should be able to advise you on the probable length of the case, pending no unforeseen delays or difficulties.

- ∽ You should be made aware of the various kinds of relief it is possible for you to seek in court (see Chapter 7). The word 'relief' is used to refer to the matters that you are asking the court to consider granting you, such as:

◆ maintenance and lump sum payments;

◆ access to and custody of your children;

◆ property division and ownership of the family home;

◆ occupation of the family home;

◆ pension rights; and

◆ succession rights.

~ A solicitor is obliged to give you an estimate of costs in writing at an early stage in the process or at least should set out the methods of charging if it is not possible to give you an accurate estimate of the final costs. It may be good practice on the part of your solicitor to provide you with detailed terms of trading or terms of reference, which could include such things as:

◆ the name, address and contact details of the legal firm, and the solicitor who will be responsible for handling your case;

◆ their place and hours of business; and

◆ the professional fee you will be charged, which normally does not include the following:

1. VAT (at 21 per cent);

2. administration costs, such as letters, faxes, telephone calls, consultations with you either in person or by telephone, photocopying, postage, commissioner for oaths' fees (when swearing documents), travelling expenses, search fees, etc;

3. the barrister's fees, which are usually quoted separately (consultations with your barrister should be included in the barrister's quote);

4. you may still be liable to pay a fee for the day, or part of a day, when a solicitor turns up with you in court and the case is adjourned to another day (my solicitor, barrister and I turned up in court on three separate occasions when the case was postponed until another day).

The terms of reference should also tell you what the professional fees cover (including the number of court appearances included in the estimate) and give you an estimation of the length of time your case is likely take.

∼ You are entitled to request periodic statements showing the status of your account.

∼ If a solicitor's fees are going to be in excess of the amount outlined in his/her initial correspondence with you, you should be informed, in writing, of the revised professional fee and the reasons for the change. Legally, a solicitor may find it slightly more difficult to recover fees against you if you have not been provided with an estimate of costs.

~ Solicitors are not allowed to charge you on a percentage basis of any award you may receive.

~ Providing a client with a statement of the terms of reference is good practice and something you should request. You should take the time to read the document and jot down any questions you may have. You should always ask your solicitor about hidden costs (i.e. if there are likely to be any other expenses that have not been outlined). Be sure you know what you are getting for your money.

Know what it is you want to achieve

To err is to be human, and we are all human. No advice is going to be 100 per cent correct. While the solicitors are the professionals, having both the legal knowledge and practical experience to know what happens in court, what the law allows for and what is most likely to happen, they cannot tell you exactly what to expect nor what you will achieve. At the end of the day, that comes down to the judge. The solicitor will help your barrister to prepare your case and will prepare you for the possible outcomes of the court case. A barrister cannot do a good job without a good foundation, and that foundation depends on how well the solicitor briefs the barrister.

The role of a solicitor is to work for you. Remember, you are paying him/her, which means that, in effect, you are the employer. Remember too that, if you were to buy something in a shop that was faulty, you would take it back.

Whatever decision is made by a court at the end of your case, it is a decision you will live with for the rest of your life. Your solicitor, on the other hand, will walk away and get a good night's sleep no matter what the outcome. While a solicitor may give you advice, it is up to you whether or not you choose to take it. Do not always presume that your solicitor will come up with every possible angle. If there are alternative solutions that, if awarded in court, you would be happy to live with, you should make your solicitor aware of them. Solicitors do not always think of everything and may not necessarily be able to see things from your perspective. When I started out on my journey towards separation, the crèche costs for my child were running at IR£200 a month. Two and a half years later, they were in excess of €800 a month. Your needs today may be different from your needs tomorrow, so make sure you try to plan ahead at least a little.

Also, what matters to one person may not matter to another. One person may be keen to remain in the family home and receive no maintenance, while another may be happy to leave the family home but may not be able to survive without maintenance payments. Every case is different. Be sure to make your solicitor aware of what it is you are hoping to achieve financially from a settlement and of what your needs are.

A solicitor acts for you and is a qualified intermediary on your behalf and, as s/he is retained by you to act for you, s/he is legally obliged to take instructions from you. You cannot instruct a solicitor to do anything which breaks the law nor to withhold any information relevant to the case that they are obliged to disclose. They will not act against the law nor will they mislead the court. A solicitor should follow the instructions of a client, but always within the confines of the law. They should advise you as to the best course of action for you, but, if you believe another course would be better, they can then proceed accordingly, providing this falls within the confines of the law and the legal system. Solicitors may withdraw their services if a client does not follow their advice. Moreover, they should withdraw if they are expected to compromise their position as an officer of the court.

What to do if you are not happy with your solicitor

When you hire a solicitor, s/he goes on record for you, which effectively means they are now officially acting on your behalf, both when negotiating with the opposing legal team and at a court appearance. If you are not happy with your solicitor and feel you are not working well together, then essentially you have two options: either manage your solicitor better or change your solicitor. As in every other area of life, not all professional relationships work either.

I have noticed that, once a solicitor is hired, many people are reluctant to change, even if they are unhappy with the service they are receiving. They may worry about how it will make them appear in court to have changed their legal representation. They can also feel that it is better the devil you know: what if they change their solicitor and the next one is no improvement on this one? Whatever the case, you should not be afraid to say if you are not happy. However, if you really do not feel confident in your solicitor, you should consider moving on. Why pay for something you are not happy with? Find a new solicitor, go for an initial consultation and get a second opinion. We have all returned goods that we are not happy with to shops, and a solicitor, as a service provider, is no different.

There is a difference, however, in not being happy with the advice you are given because you simply do not like what you are hearing and not being happy because you feel the solicitor is not adequately advising you of all possible remedies. Take some time to make sure you know the difference between the two. If your legal bills are climbing and your results are not, ask why and then reassess the situation. If you have difficulty in communicating with your solicitor, the chances are they are not really listening to you.

There are some things you should know if you choose to change your solicitor during the process:

- Once the fees and outlays of your first solicitor have been paid, the file actually belongs to you and should be released to you in full.

- If you move from one solicitor to another, your new solicitor will require sight of your previous legal correspondence. Most solicitors will not release your file to you until all outstanding bills have been settled. You should, however, have copies of all legal correspondence to date, as your solicitor should always send you a copy of all written correspondence undertaken on your behalf.

- At the initial consultation, your new solicitor will ensure that you understand your obligation to pay the bill due for work done by the previous solicitor.

~ Your previous solicitor may opt to accept an undertaking from your new solicitor to discharge the fees before releasing your file to them. In this case, all outlays should be refunded to the first solicitor immediately.

~ If you dismiss your solicitor or s/he withdraws, and if the legal proceedings are already issued and s/he is on record, s/he must bring a motion to come off record, which is served on both you as the client and the other party. If you simply change solicitor, the new solicitor will issue a notice of change of solicitor. This is served on the previous solicitor and on the solicitor for the other party.

~ You should also contact the Law Society, the solicitors' governing body. In most areas of law, if you have a complaint about the conduct of your solicitor, either in relation to his/her handling of a case or in relation to the bill, you can refer it to the Law Society for scrutiny. However, during my time seeking a judicial separation, it was impossible to bring a complaint to the Law Society because of the in-camera law governing family law in Ireland. The current winds of change will hopefully bring about a variation in the in-camera rule, and this may be something that will become possible. (For further information on this, see 'The in-camera rule' section on pages 76–77.)

A final thought

If you find yourself in an adversarial situation, taking the time to find the right solicitor is of paramount importance. Time spent wisely now may save you time and money in the future. While most solicitors are good and provide an excellent service, one does sometimes hear of the few that don't. Some may be somewhat lethargic in their approach to a case where speed is of the essence, who concentrate on the here and now without planning for you and your potential future needs.

Remember, it is your case. You know what is important to you, but your solicitor may not, so you need to ensure that you give him/her that information. When you have found the right solicitor, take the time and trouble to listen to him/her. S/he will have no axe to grind.

[3]

BARRISTERS

When I started out on the road to separation, I thought that, once I found the right solicitor for me, I would no longer need to think about my legal representation. I was not aware that I may need a barrister. I was also unaware as to the difference in the service they provided as opposed to that of my solicitor, and the additional cost of hiring one. When I realised I would need a barrister, this choice proved more challenging than finding the right solicitor. I spoke to other people who had been through the same process and tried to carry out some research of my own on how to go about finding one. Eventually, I received a recommendation from a friend and I followed up on this. The solicitor I had chosen to represent me had also worked with this barrister on previous occasions. In fact, clients would not usually select their own barrister but would work with one recommended by their solicitor (i.e. one with whom the solicitor has an established working relationship).

How barristers practise

Barristers are members of the Bar Council of Ireland and, in a way, belong to the upper echelons of the legal profession. Barristers are often referred to as 'counsel'. There are two types of counsel: junior counsel (BL) and senior counsel (SC). If you take a walk through the courtrooms of Ireland, the barristers are the ones who wear white wigs and black gowns, whereas solicitors just wear business attire.

There are over 1,000 barristers practising law in Ireland. The majority of barristers are junior counsel and senior counsel make up just a small percentage. Senior counsel are more experienced in their area of law and are usually a great deal more expensive than junior counsel. Do not let that worry you, as many junior counsel are very talented in their area and can make just as good a case as a senior counsel. Only very rarely would a senior counsel be retained in a circuit court case.

Unlike solicitors, barristers do not belong to a legal firm; they are individual people in private practice. They operate from the courtrooms and may have offices nearby. The roles of your solicitor and barrister are different and do not generally overlap. The rule of thumb is that solicitors deal with the day-to-day preparation of a case and the necessary documents and barristers provide specialist advice and are more practised in courtroom procedures.

Why do you need a barrister?

Barristers are very specialised legal advisers and are experts in making representations in a courtroom (i.e. to the judge). They act independently of solicitors and are trained to advise clients on the pros and cons or strengths and weaknesses of a particular case. Given that their career is spent in and out of courtrooms, they are well qualified to advise you on the potential outcome of your case and to give you clear advice on what it is you should be seeking and what it is they would hope to achieve on your behalf.

Barristers are the people who act on your behalf in a courtroom. They will prepare the arguments in relation to your case and decide how these will be presented in court. The barrister will be responsible for the verbal presentation of your case in court and your solicitor will do most of the preparatory work, including collecting and providing all the paperwork and answering any questions your barrister may have. Barristers are not involved with day-to-day communication with the opposing legal team. That is the role of your solicitor, who will, however, be acting in conjunction with your barrister.

Your consultations with your barrister are private, much as with your solicitor. Unless your barrister becomes aware that you are planning to do something that is against the law, all the information s/he receives about you and discusses with you is confidential. Your barrister will act in your best interests and give you the best advice possible about your particular case. Barristers are independent professional people and, like your solicitor, will have no conflict of interest in dealing with your case. If the barrister has already met or advised your spouse, s/he will not take your case. Your barrister must present your case on your behalf in a way that will achieve the best result for you. If your barrister feels that the legal advice you have received from your solicitor is incorrect or inadequate, s/he will see that you are properly informed. Your solicitor will select a barrister who is experienced in the relevant area of law. Obviously, if you, as a client, do not like the barrister retained by your solicitor, s/he can be changed, but it is usual practice to rely on the experience of your solicitor in the selection.

How to find the best barrister for you

The most common ways for people to find the right barrister are by selecting one by reputation or through a personal recommendation, or by selecting one on the recommendation of their solicitor.

The Bar Council of Ireland, the barristers' governing body, has a database with full contact details for all barristers and what their specialist area is. You can search this database and, according to their speciality, put together a list of possible barristers. You can then discuss with your solicitor which of these would be best suited to your case.

In most cases, barristers do not deal with the client directly; they will take instruction from the client's solicitor. Your solicitor will probably have at least one barrister that they are used to working with. If your solicitor has a proven track record in the area of family law, s/he will probably use a barrister who is particularly good in that area. If, however, the barrister recommended by your solicitor is not the one you wish to use, you can ask your solicitor to approach the barrister you do wish to use to see if s/he is free to advise you or represent you in court.

A private individual does not usually approach a barrister directly. Your solicitor will retain one on your behalf. The solicitor will act as an intermediary and deal with the barrister for you. In this way, the solicitor always has all the information relating to your case.

When do you meet with your barrister?

A solicitor may retain a barrister on your behalf to provide nothing more than advice. You may be considering alternative methods of reaching a solution, such as a separation agreement, and your solicitor could take advice from a barrister as to what they consider fair in relation to your case, or on a particular area of your case which is of concern to you. If there are unusual aspects to your case, your solicitor may also seek advice from a barrister regarding how best to handle these.

If your case is going to result in a day in court, it is usual practice for there to be a pre-hearing consultation between yourself, your barrister and your solicitor. However, if your case is fairly straightforward in family law terms, you may well only meet the barrister on the day of the court appearance. In this eventuality, the barrister will have been briefed by your solicitor. While this may be all that is required in a straightforward case, it could be quite disconcerting to have someone you have never met speak on your behalf. If a meeting is arranged with your barrister, it is more usual for this to occur prior to the day your case is scheduled. At such a meeting, the barrister will explain how s/he intends to present your case on the day and will discuss which areas of the case may be focused on by the opposing side. Any outstanding questions will also be cleared up.

How to manage your barrister – establishing the facts

You will have considerably less contact with your barrister than with your solicitor, which is why it is so important to have a good professional relationship with your solicitor. It is equally important that your solicitor has a good relationship with your barrister. The solicitor will gather information from you and pass it on to the barrister. S/he must ensure that your barrister is fully aware of all the details of your case and will instruct him/her on how you wish to proceed. Be sure to tell your solicitor if there is something you want your barrister to know.

What you should expect from your barrister

Your barrister will prepare the documents that will be used in court on the day, such as your motion and grounding affidavit. The barrister's understanding of your case will be reflected in the paperwork. Always take the time to read through any paperwork prepared for you to make sure it is accurate. It should fully reflect your position as you see it and clearly state what you hope to achieve. If you want to seek the relief of the court, you must ask this of the court, in which case your barrister may include other items in the paperwork that you have not specified. An example of this would be an order for costs (a request to the court to determine who is responsible for the legal costs in relation to your case): if you have had to go to court to seek enforcement of a maintenance order, for instance, your barrister may request that an award be made instructing the opposing side to bear the costs as the court action has resulted from a breach of the original court order by the other party.

The barrister's job is to present arguments on your behalf to enable the court to reach a decision on your case. The barrister will not mislead the court. You may also feel that you want to include more in your affidavit than your barrister thinks wise. If this is the case, s/he will explain the pros and cons of lengthy paperwork versus short and to the point.

When your barrister is speaking for you, you are not allowed to interrupt and any attempt to do so will not be viewed favourably by the court. The most you can do is pass a note to your barrister or solicitor if something that is said is untrue or inaccurate. Your legal team should be fully aware of all the aspects of your case, but they are not privy to every little detail, nor will every little detail be considered. They are just interested in the points that are relevant to their arguments.

You should (or at least I did) expect the following things from your barrister:

~ You should expect to receive honest legal advice about your case, explained in an open and concise way.

~ Do not expect your barrister to tell you what to say in court. You will be told, however, how to deal with the courtroom situation: speaking slowly and clearly, addressing the judge, keeping your answers concise, etc.

~ The barrister is not there to take pot shots at your estranged spouse. If there is clear evidence relating to certain actions of your spouse, the barrister may use it, but s/he will not make false accusations.

~ Barristers will not lie on your behalf. They are officers of the court and are bound by the ethics of the court.

~ Barristers will not deliberately mislead the court.

~ Once you begin giving your testimony, your barrister, and indeed your solicitor, cannot talk to you about your evidence (if, for example, there is a break in your case either for lunch or at the end of the day). They can only speak with you when your testimony is complete.

~ Always make sure you read thoroughly any paperwork that is being presented in court. Do not presume it is 100 per cent correct. You will be required to swear that any documents used in court are true statements of your case after your solicitor has explained the contents. Take the time to listen to the explanations.

Know your needs and what it is you want to achieve

The best advice I can give is always to be honest with your barrister. The greater the barrister's understanding of your case, the greater his/her chance of helping you. If you have a clear idea of what it is you want to achieve, you should make your barrister aware of this. Barristers are usually very frank and, if they think a point a client is trying to make will not stand up in court or is not worth arguing, they will say so. If the barrister thinks you have no chance of achieving what it is you hope to achieve, s/he will tell you. Something that makes sense to you, on an emotional basis, may have no standing in a court of law and your barrister will make you aware of this. This may be hard to hear, but better to hear it now and come to terms with it than leave yourself open to the unexpected on the day in court.

Before you meet with your barrister, it is very useful to write down all the points you want to make. Address all these issues with your barrister and check them off your list as you go. If your barrister explains something to you and you don't understand, be sure to say so. The more unanswered questions you have, the more nervous you will be about going to court. The more quantifiable answers you have, the easier it will be to at least be prepared for potential possible outcomes. It is important that you both have the same set of expectations before going to court. Be very clear and concise with your barrister. If there is something that you will or will not be flexible about, be sure to say so. Remember, barristers are there to serve the client's needs, not their own agenda.

What to do if you are not happy with your barrister

Dealing with your barrister may seem like a daunting task, and indeed it can be. I took the view that, as I was not a barrister or a solicitor, I was not conversant with the legal aspects of my case, just the human aspect, the side that was personal to me. I was simply paying them and hiring them as professionals to provide me with a service. I believed that I should feel as comfortable asking for information as they were comfortable being paid for it. You should not feel daunted by the legal precedents a barrister may put before you or the advice they give you. Just as with your solicitor, the barrister will walk away from the case at the end of the day and you will be left to deal with the decision of the court. You will know what is important to you and what it is you want to at least try to achieve, but, if the barrister advises you that what you are looking for is unreasonable, you must listen, as it is this expert advice that you are paying for. S/he may come up with possible alternative options, in which case take the time to think about any such suggestions. You can always advise the barrister at a later date, through your solicitor, if you want to take his/her advice or not. If you strongly disagree with the barrister's suggested course of action, instruct him/her to pursue the settlement you wish to look for. Even barristers can be surprised at the judgments passed down by the courts. However, there can be no guarantees, so do consider their advice.

If you meet with your barrister and are unhappy, for whatever reason, with the level of service you receive, you should discuss it with your solicitor. Sometimes the advice offered by a barrister can seem hard, and you may hear things you do not like. This is not to say that the advice is incorrect, merely that you are not comfortable with it. You must be prepared to accept that not all your expectations may be met by the court or indeed heard by the court.

If you are dissatisfied with a barrister, a new barrister can be retained on your behalf. Again, this will be subject to the first barrister being paid for work that has been carried out to date (including consultations).

It is important, no matter what the advice you receive from your barrister, that you walk away feeling that they:

- listened to what you had to say;
- had a good understanding of the facts of your case;
- had a clear understanding of what it is you hope to achieve by going to court;
- answered any questions you had in a manner that you understood; and
- explained their role in the process.

After you appear in court, time permitting, sit down for a quick debrief with your barrister. If you are unhappy about how you were represented, now is not the time for silence – now is the time to speak up.

Settlement meetings

Your solicitor, on your instructions, may contact the other party to see if s/he is willing to meet to discuss reaching an agreement without going to court. Such a meeting will usually take place at the barrister's rooms with you and your solicitor in attendance. You will not be in the same room as your estranged spouse or his/her legal team. They will usually be in the office of their own barrister and your barrister will go back and forth between the two offices, either informing the other side of an offer you want to make or informing you of an offer your spouse wishes to make to you. This can be a difficult time and you may feel under pressure to make a decision in relation to an offer, which is not always the best way to make a good decision. Your barrister will advise you as to whether it is a fair and reasonable offer, but they cannot force you to accept it if you are unwilling to do so. Your barrister may talk with the opposing side's barrister if they think the case can be settled. S/he will not, however, reveal any confidential information to the other side, except with your express permission. Your barrister will tell you anything that has been discussed. If an offer has been made, you do not necessarily have to make a decision there and then. An offer can be left open for a period of time prior to the court date, so you can go away and take some time to think it over. You can always go back with a counter offer, rather than a definitive yes or no.

What if the barrister has another case being heard in the family courts on the same day?

It did not dawn on me until just before we went to court that my barrister could have another client in the family courts on the same day as me. Barristers do not decide the date on which a case will be heard; that is the decision of the court. When a date is being set or applied for, a barrister may make the court aware that they already have another case listed for that day and so seek an alternative date. However, as I found going through the court system, not everything always runs according to schedule. Cases can get cancelled or may run over their projected time, which in turn may affect other cases scheduled for the same barrister.

In the event that this happens, your barrister may have to stay with the other case. An application can be made to the courts for an adjournment of your case, particularly if it is complex, or, alternatively, your barrister can assist your solicitor in finding a replacement barrister to deal with your case on the day. Barristers may also have what is known as a 'devil', who may be able to present your case in court on the day. A devil is a recently qualified barrister who is gaining court experience from an established and more experienced barrister.

Costs

While I would love to be able to quote you an exact figure of how much your barrister's fees will amount to, this is simply not possible. The cost of your barrister, like your solicitor, will depend on a number of things. The more complicated your case and the longer it takes, the more expensive it will be. The cost is also affected by the time the barrister spends on your case, both in meeting with you, preparing any paperwork and going to court (including time spent at court waiting for your case to be heard, or if the case is adjourned), and their level of experience.

The terms of reference you received from your solicitor usually covers the solicitor's own costs, and the costs of a barrister are in addition to that. Because your solicitor retains the barrister on your behalf, payment to the barrister is made through your solicitor. Your solicitor should provide you with an estimate of costs for your barrister.

Barristers do not charge hourly or daily rates. Their costs are compiled according to the amount of meetings, paperwork and brief fees. These vary depending on the court involved and its complexity. A barrister can provide an estimate of costs based on how long s/he thinks your case will last and the time needed to prepare for it. This again is an approximate sum. Many variable factors can arise, such as additional hearings, postponements, or simply that the case takes longer than was originally envisaged. Such time delays can be governed by how willing the opposing party is to settle or how often either you, or they, go to court. Either side has leave to apply to go back to court to appeal or seek new reliefs, but this cannot be foreseen when estimating fees. However, expect the total cost to be in the thousands, not hundreds.

Summary

Finding a barrister is yet another layer in what is already for many a truly difficult process. This is no time to leave things unsaid. Remember, your legal team is there to make sure you receive sound, honest and up-to-date legal advice and to give you the best possible representation in court. Hard as it is when dealing with such an emotional issue, try to hear what is being said to you and ensure that your representatives are also aware of what it is you want, what is important to you and why you want a particular settlement. If there are any other options you would be willing to accept, make sure you let them know – as talented as many may be, they are not mind-readers.

Keep a notebook for meetings with your solicitor and barrister. Use the same notebook for all meetings and in that way you can keep all the notes you make at meetings and all the points you want to make in one place. It is a good idea to write down the answers you receive too, either during the meeting or straight afterwards. This will mean that, when the emotions have subsided, you will be able to read any points that have been made in a calmer light at a time when you may be more ready to deal with what has been said. It will also help prevent confusion and misunderstandings.

[4]

REPRESENTING YOURSELF – ACTING LAY LITIGANT

Sitting at the back of a courtroom, hearing my barrister make legal representations on my behalf, was an incredibly strange experience. I was grateful to have both my solicitor and barrister with me, providing me with a buffer at a time when I felt ill-equipped to deal with the situation at hand. I had a sick feeling in the pit of my stomach and was so stressed I was actually laughing with nervousness and total disbelief that this was happening to me.

Sitting in silence at the back of a courtroom – you are not allowed speak unless called upon to do so – hearing a professional and impartial person speaking on your behalf feels a bit like picking over the bones of a dead carcass, only this one may still have some life left in it, as all the issues have yet to be put to bed. The barrister may refer to some of the most personal things in relation to your marriage and this can affect different people in different ways. One person may be glad the barrister is

44

there, grateful to have professional help shielding him/her from the experience and dealing with it on his/her behalf. Another person may sit there listening to the legal arguments and want to stand up and scream that the way s/he is being portrayed is completely wrong and everyone is missing the point, that the things that matter to him/her have not even been mentioned and a decision has been passed down that is not reflective of his/her situation.

At the start of my journey, I would never in a million years have considered or been open to the possibility of representing myself. It was too grave a situation and would be too distressing to even contemplate putting forward legal arguments on my own behalf. I had met one other person who had represented himself and, if it had not been for him, I would not have looked at the option. My journey through the legal process took a long time and, with each successive court appearance, my requirement for a buffer lessened, the arguments became easier and I felt that I could do it with my eyes closed.

This chapter has been written for people who are open to representing themselves. Where you are on the emotional yardstick, and the issues involved, will influence whether or not you should, or are capable of, representing yourself. So, let us look at some facts first.

Who can represent you in court?

A solicitor, a barrister or a barrister's 'devil' can represent you in court, but you can also represent yourself. A solicitor, unless yours is a very straightforward case, will usually be reluctant, if not unwilling, to represent you in court. Such is not really their remit, although they legally may do so. A barrister makes a living out of representing clients in court. Apart from these options, you can, and are legally entitled to, represent yourself.

A solicitor will usually only represent a client in the district court. It would be more unusual for a solicitor to represent you in the circuit and high courts, although it does happen more now than it used to. It would also be very rare for a barrister to represent a client in the district court.

Pros and cons when choosing the lay litigant route

'Lay litigant' is the term used to refer to someone who chooses to represent him or herself.

There are a number of pros and cons involved in choosing to go lay litigant.

THE PROS

~ It is significantly cheaper.

~ In some cases, only you will know the real issues in relation to your case and, if speaking from the heart, you may be the best person to be heard on the subject.

~ You will have total involvement from the outset.

~ If the issues are not contentious, it is not as emotionally draining.

~ The court will not necessarily be more sympathetic towards someone who is representing himself or herself, but they may give more latitude when you are making arguments as you are not a professional in the area.

THE CONS

~ You are obliged to complete all the necessary paperwork in relation to either your application or in response to a notice served upon you.

~ There are certain protocols regarding filing paperwork and regarding the notice periods according to which you and the opposing side are entitled to receive and serve paperwork. A case may not be heard if these have not been complied with.

~ You will be responsible for dealing with the solicitors and for presenting arguments in opposition to the barrister/solicitor for the other side.

~ Completing the necessary paperwork is fairly time-consuming, and you will also have to find the time to lodge the necessary paperwork in the courts (usually done in person) and serve them on the opposing side (which is usually done by registered post).

~ You will be responsible for tracking all documentation in relation to your case and producing it on the day in court.

~ If the paperwork is inaccurately completed or inadequate material is provided, the case may be adjourned to another day to allow you to rectify the situation, which can cause even further delays and expense.

~ You will no longer have a buffer, a barrister or solicitor who can deal impartially with the case. You need to ask yourself if you are able just to focus on the bigger picture.

~ If it all goes wrong on the day and an order is made that you are unhappy with, unless you wish to appeal it, you will be bound by the decision of the court.

~ You need to be sure that you are best placed to argue from a legal perspective, as opposed to an emotional one.

Factors to consider before going lay litigant

~ How complex are the issues in your case?

~ How will you deal with the unexpected or with legal arguments from the other side?

~ Have you the time to prepare and serve all the required paperwork?

~ Are you familiar with the courts and how they work (who speaks first, counter arguments and the process on the day)?

~ Do you feel comfortable addressing issues which may be highly charged and personal?

~ Are you confident that you can remain objective on the day?

~ Have you worked out the worst-case scenario if it all goes pear-shaped and can you live with this?

~ Do you have anything to lose? Can you walk out of the courtroom in a worse position than when you walked in?

~ Have you had the benefit of legal advice about the issues involved?

~ Can you identify any arguments that the opposing side may use to make their case in court on the day?

~ Are you objective enough to see the case from your spouse's point of view and would you feel confident dealing with any objections s/he may have?

~ Is this your first time in court?

~ Have you heard a similar case argued by your legal team?

I realise the above points are a lot to think about. To my mind, the deciding factor should be the complexity of the issues relevant to your particular case. If there are too many issues – such as the family home, maintenance, seeking disclosure of paperwork, access – to deal with on the day, the chances are you may get snowed under, lose focus and concentrate on the things that you are more emotionally connected with. If what is important to you does not come up until the end of the hearing, you may be too stressed or unfocused when dealing with the other issues, and this could cost you dearly. If, on the other hand, there is just one issue to deal with, it is easier to remain focused. If your case is quite complex, with a number of issues to be decided, I would strongly encourage you to seek legal advice and consider having legal representation.

What if I change my mind and require formal representation?

If you embark on the process of representing yourself but subsequently change your mind, you can do so. The fact that you have started on the process of lay litigant does not mean you are bound to it for the rest of your case. If you feel that the issues are too substantive, too emotional or that you do not have a clear understanding of what is required – and, more importantly, what is at stake – I would urge you to seek legal representation. If you find yourself in a courtroom and sinking fast, you should ask the judge for an adjournment for the purpose of obtaining legal representation. There is no shame in changing your mind. If you decide to hire a legal team, at least you will feel comfortable with your decision, knowing that you have tried the alternative.

What is the attitude of the courts towards those who act lay litigant?

The courtroom is sacrosanct. You are entering the domain of a judge, where s/he has the power to make a wide range of orders either against you or on your behalf. You should accord due respect to the court at all times. Family courts try to be the most compassionate of all courts. These courts have been set up in such a way that the process will be less daunting and will be sensitive to the people who find themselves in need of them, but they are still courtrooms. Judges may be slightly more lenient in the way they deal with a person who is representing him/herself. They will endeavour to ensure that you are comfortable and that you understand all the points of law being made and their ramifications. While a solicitor and barrister are officers of the court and are bound by a certain code of conduct and ethics, you are approaching the process from a different standpoint. By this I mean that you may say something that a professional would not, and the court may allow you some leeway in this as you are not a professional in the field. They will not, however, let you have a free rein and will curtail you if you digress from the point.

You should be mindful of how you behave and respectful to the court at all times. Courtesy is never wasted and in this instance it will be expected.

What are my obligations if I represent myself?

It is not just a case of showing up on the day and saying what you like. If you are representing yourself as the applicant, you will have to prepare the notice of motion, service of motion and grounding affidavit, giving details of why you sought the court date and the reliefs you are looking for. If you are the respondent, you will have to prepare and file (lodge with the courts and the other side) your replying affidavit (an affidavit responding to the applicant's affidavit) with your response to the issues raised by the other side. You are also free to bring up issues of your own through your affidavit and to seek reliefs. The following is a list of things you may potentially have to do:

- Prepare the necessary paperwork (whether you are the applicant or respondent).
- Serve the necessary paperwork.
- Deal with the opposing legal team.
- Make arguments in court on the day.
- Follow up with the courts to obtain a copy of an order if one is made.
- Follow up with the opposing side's solicitor if s/he is ordered to do something.

Can I still take legal advice if representing myself?

You can still take legal advice if you are representing yourself, and I would strongly advise that you do. The further you are along the process and the more familiar you become with the way it operates, then hopefully the less advice you will need. The amount of advice you need will depend to a large extent on how complex the issues are that you are dealing with. However, if it is your maiden voyage, I would urge that you do take legal advice, as it is not going to worsen your position to do so and it may in fact greatly enhance your situation.

Why represent yourself?

Different people have different reasons for doings things. I can only speak for myself. I had reached a point where I was tired – tired of all the legal argument and tired of having a buffer. After a couple of years and more court cases than I care to remember, I got to the stage where I no longer required one, where I knew I was more than capable of standing in a courtroom on my own. It actually got to the point where it became important to me to do so. By then I knew I could be objective enough to deal with the issues on the table without them getting clouded by anything else. On the practical side, the fact that I was paying a mortgage, a crèche bill and all the other household bills and raising my child on my own did not leave me the resources to pay ongoing legal fees. In fact, they had become a luxury I could no longer afford. In hindsight I can honestly say that it was one of the best experiences for me in the entire process – it validated me as a person – but only because the timing was right and it was something I was comfortable doing.

Can you represent yourself if you have legal representation?

If you have retained someone to represent you, you cannot change your mind suddenly and stand up in court and represent yourself. If, however, you have used legal representation and then decided that, as the substantive issues have been awarded earlier in the process, you can deal with any future or remaining issues, you can have your solicitor and barrister come off record and formally go on the record as representing yourself.

Making your arguments in court on the day

I am not saying that representing yourself will be a walk in the park. It's a bit like sitting an exam: you never really feel comfortable until you get started; the waiting around beforehand is not the most pleasant of experiences. Outlined below is my advice on what, in my opinion, is the best way to approach the process of preparing for the court case and presenting your case in court.

How to prepare before the court case
Read the affidavit of the other side and your own really well. Know everything they contain so there are no surprises on the day. If an issue is not listed in the affidavit, it makes it nigh on impossible to deal with it on the day.

~ Each side is entitled to receive notice of the reason why they will have to appear in court. If the opposing side brings up something which you were not notified of in the affidavit, you could hardly be expected to deal with it on the day. Focus on the issues in hand. New issues should not be dealt with on the day, only those that are outlined in the affidavit.

~ Sit down and work out your replies to each of the points that have been raised. Know what it is you want to say and the points you wish to make. Try to do so as succinctly as possible. The less said, the less to be argued against. Stick to the point and don't wander into any other areas.

~ Depending on the issues, it is useful to come up with alternative solutions that you would be willing to accept. While judges will make decisions by listening to the two sides of an argument, they will also consider any possible alternatives. Write any alternatives that would be acceptable to you on one sheet of paper (keep it simple) and, if the need arises on the day, hand it to the judge for consideration. A judge may be happy to consider a third alternative that is a good compromise between what both people want.

~ Write notes to help you on the day, so that, if your mind goes blank, you can refer to something you have prepared previously to help you get through.

~ Writing everything down will ensure that you forget none of the points you want to make.

~ If it will help, run through what you are going to say with a friend. Do not simply describe the content, but actually stand up in a room and say your piece aloud in front of someone. If you have already said it to someone else, you will be familiar with how it sounds and it will slide off the tongue more smoothly on the day. If you are not comfortable doing this with a friend, stand in front of a mirror and make your points aloud in private. Your courtroom appearance on the day should not be the first time you verbalise what you have to say.

~ Remember the reason you are in court and focus on that. Think of nothing else.

~ Do not get involved in any debate with the other side before your case is heard, as it will only throw you off base. If they want to settle, listen to what they have to say and walk away to think about it.

~ Bring a friend with you if possible, someone who can remain objective and is not emotionally involved. It is nice to have the support of someone else.

~ They say you should never study the night before an exam. So it is with a court case. Take some time out to relax. It will pay off in the long run.

How to deal with the case in the courtroom

~ Speak slowly and clearly. When you feel you have made your point, stop talking and move on to the next one.

~ Try not to fidget – it distracts people.

~ Do not let the other side undermine you. Most solicitors or barristers would feel far more confident facing a lay litigant, as they may think, given the difference in experience between you, that they will walk rings around you. However, this is not always the case. Someone who is actually involved in the case can often make a more authentic plea than someone who is not.

~ You are not a legal professional, so do not try to become one overnight. Be open and honest about who you are: a private individual making arguments on their own behalf. Speak openly and honestly and in a respectful manner to the judge. If you have put the groundwork into your affidavit, stick to the points you bring up in it. Do not try to climb on to the legal playing field; leave that to the professionals. Concentrate on making your own points at your own level.

~ Write down any points that come up in court as you go along, then, if you need to reply to them, you have them all listed in front of you.

~ Do not, under any circumstances, interrupt the judge when s/he is speaking. If you have something additional you want to say, ask the judge if you can speak.

~ In the district court, a judge is simply addressed as 'Judge'. In the circuit court, a judge is addressed as 'My lord'. This applies whether the judge is male or female.

~ Make eye contact when speaking to the judge. Do not look at the other side unless you need to. Stay focused on your own issues. If the other side makes a point you disagree with, write it down and deal with it when it is your turn to address the court.

~ If you hear something you do not like, you must deal with it objectively.

~ Do not focus on your ex-spouse; focus on yourself. S/he may have a legal team looking after him/her, but you just look after yourself.

~ Do not adopt the terminology of the opposing side. You have probably never referred to your estranged spouse in formal language, so continue to use his/her Christian name now.

My top twelve tips

1. Remain objective and focused on the case in hand. Do not cloud the issues with other matters.

2. Take your time.

3. Do not try to make groundbreaking legal arguments – stick to the points in hand.

4. You are not a solicitor or barrister, so do not portray yourself as one. Present your points simply and honestly without any pretensions.

5. At all times be respectful to the court, both in the way you speak and the way you dress. There is no need to rush out and buy a brand-new suit, but make sure that you look presentable – do not show up in an old pair of jeans or your

gardening clothes! If you don't take your case seriously, why should anyone else?

6. If you do not understand something, be sure to say so. You can ask for clarification on any point.

7. Be prepared – have all the necessary paperwork with you. Always have three copies – one for you, one for the judge and one for the opposing side – and always have originals where relevant. Bring any other paperwork you may need, whether it is a bill, a medical note or whatever. If the originals have to be handed in, you can always ask the court clerk for them back later.

8. Forget about the opposing side – and ignore how much paperwork they have. I know one person who went to court with just one piece of paper, while the opposing side had so many files that it took two people to carry them. The one piece of paper did it and was enough to win on the issues. It is quality, not quantity, that counts.

9. Always take legal advice, where possible, on any aspects of your case you do not understand.

10. Remember that the courts are there to help you, so try not to aggravate them.

11. If you have to deal with correspondence from the opposing side's solicitor prior to the case, do not let it intimidate you. Never reply to a letter if you are upset or angry – wait until you feel calm and

objective. Do not be derogatory, even if they are, and keep it brief, even if they don't. The court makes the decisions, not the opposing solicitor, so save your arguments for where they belong – in the courtroom. Keep all correspondence as concise as possible and craft responses in a conciliatory fashion. Be careful about what you commit to paper. Remember, all correspondence between both sides can be produced in court.

12. Practise what you are going to say beforehand – preparation is the key.

[5]

LEGAL AID

One of the biggest hurdles that people seeking a judicial separation through the court system face is the sheer expense of it all. When you take the potential joint costs of both parties, it can equate to a sizeable deposit on a home. Take a hypothetical situation as an example: if both parties are living in an area where the price of purchasing a home averages at around €250,000 and each party's legal bills come to approximately €18,000 (which can easily happen in a case where several court appearances are required), when you combine the two legal bills you could have a deposit of €36,000 – just over 14% of the asking price for the house. Finding the deposit for a home is one of the major financial outlays faced by most couples. This demonstrates the scale of the potential legal costs of separating.

If you do not have the resources to take on this kind of legal battle, you may want to consider the possibility of legal aid as a way of securing legal representation.

The Legal Aid Board

The Legal Aid Board provides legal advice and legal aid in civil cases to persons who satisfy the requirements of the Civil Legal Aid Act (1995). This primarily means that a person's means must be below a certain limit and that there must be merit to the case.

Legal advice

Legal advice is advice given to you about your situation from a legal point of view by someone who is qualified to give you such advice.

Legal aid

The question of legal aid arises outside and after legal advice and is based on taking a case forward for consideration by a court. It constitutes representation by a solicitor or barrister through the court system.

How do I seek legal aid/advice?

You can call into any of the law centres listed at the end of this chapter, or telephone or write to the centre nearest to you.

How do I know if I am eligible for legal aid/advice?

Anyone applying for either aid or advice must undergo a means test. This means test will be in respect of both your income and your capital resources. The law centre staff will assess your means and your financial eligibility and, if you are eligible for legal aid, they will calculate the amount of the total contribution you will be liable to pay.

Are legal aid and legal advice free?

Legal advice and legal aid are not necessarily free. All persons who avail of either service must pay a contribution. The amount you have to pay will depend on your disposable income. The minimum income contribution for legal advice is €6 and for legal aid is €35. The maximum contribution for legal advice is €100 and for legal aid the amount will depend on a person's disposable income and the cost to the Legal Aid Board of providing legal services.

What are the financial parameters for applying for legal aid?

At the time of writing this book, an applicant for legal services must have a disposable income which does not exceed €13,000 and disposable capital which does not exceed €320,000.

How do I apply for legal aid or advice?

If you wish to apply for legal aid or advice, the Legal Aid Board will require you to complete a number of forms in order to assess the merits of your case. Making an application for legal aid does not necessarily mean that it will be granted.

Do not let the number of forms to be filled in put you off. If you do not go through the Legal Aid Board, you will not have to fill in any forms to hire a solicitor, but there can still be a lot of paperwork involved, so completing a few forms now to keep your options open is not really such a hardship. There is no such thing as a free lunch, and legal aid has some financial costs as well. However, there is a range, which at least makes it something you can budget for rather than facing the potential spiralling costs if you hire your own solicitor (outside legal aid). The law centre will assist you in completing the forms.

What are the forms I will have to complete?

If you are applying for legal aid, you must complete an application form stating the subject matter for which the legal aid or advice is being sought. This will be discussed with you at your first consultation. You will also be means-tested for legal aid. This will require you to complete a statement of means (income) form. The staff at the law centre will carry out the financial assessment in order to determine if you satisfy the financial eligibility criteria. You have to disclose your financial status to make the application.

Statement of means form

The detailed statement of means form (shown in the Appendix, page 188) will require you to disclose your total income. This income will include anything you receive in the form of wages, salary, social welfare or any other source of income that you have. However, legal aid will be granted, not on the basis of your income, but on the basis of your disposable income. In order to calculate your disposable income, you can write off certain amounts/allowances against your gross income. You should check with your nearest law centre at the time of your application what these allowances are. At the time of writing this book, the maximum amounts (in euro) that can be offset against your gross income are as follows:

Spouse/partner	€1,900
Adult and child dependants	€1,100
Accommodation costs	€4,900
Childcare per child	€1,100
Income tax	full amount
PRSI	full amount

If you require assistance in completing this form, someone from the law centre will assist you. The law centre will also require you to provide certain information, such as a copy of your latest payslip, a copy of your social welfare payment slip and a rent book or mortgage statement.

Statement of means (capital) form

You will be required to complete a statement of means form if your capital resources exceed €320,000. This form will require you to disclose your total capital assets, which can be in the form of property, a car, cash in hand and/or in the bank, investments and any other capital resources you may have. You will be allowed to offset certain debts against capital for the purposes of determining what your disposable capital is. These debts could include such things as mortgage repayments, Credit Union loans, etc.

If I pass the means test, what costs will I then incur?

If you pass the means test, there will still be some financial costs – some of which we have already addressed. You should also be aware that the Legal Aid Board is entitled, subject to certain limited exceptions, to deduct the costs it has incurred in providing legal services from any monies/property a person recovers as a result of legal services provided. Where appropriate, the board will deduct its costs and return the balance to the person who was in receipt of legal aid. The actual contribution that a person pays will be related to the cost to the board of providing legal services in your case. You should discuss this with the Legal Aid Board before your case proceeds so as to be clear what happens when your case concludes and to ensure that you are aware of any potential financial liability you may have. It is important to be clear about what your financial obligations are likely to be.

Assessing the merits of your case

Anyone applying for legal aid will undergo a merits test. In order for the Legal Aid Board to agree to take your case, once you qualify financially, the board must be satisfied that it is reasonable to take or defend the proceedings based on the merits of your case.

The board will use a number of criteria to assess the merits of your case. They will consider how likely your case is to be successful and whether any other method, other than court proceedings, would be more suitable for dealing with the issues in your case. They will probably ask if you have considered mediation. The board will measure the cost of providing legal aid against the likely benefit to the applicant if s/he is successful in the proceedings. They will also apply different levels of stringency to these tests, depending on what the proceedings are about. By this I mean that, if your case involves the welfare of a child, including issues of custody and access, they may modify the conditions of the merits test.

If starting on this journey, you should make a phone call to your local Legal Aid Board, speak with a representative of the board and, after this initial conversation, complete the required paperwork and see where it takes you.

Waiting time

The length of time it takes to have your application assessed can vary considerably between law centres, depending on the amount of applications being handled at any one time. However, it is a considerably slower process than taking out the phone book, picking a solicitor and organising your own legal representation. All things being equal, it can be many months before your application results in actual legal aid.

What if legal aid is granted?

If your application is successful and legal aid is granted, you will be issued with a Legal Aid Certificate, which will specify the legal services being offered to you. Your solicitor, who will be selected from the panel of solicitors working with the Legal Aid Board, cannot initiate or defend court proceedings for you until you do the following:

~ Sign your Legal Aid Certificate.

~ Pay the legal aid contribution specified on the certificate.

You have a period of one month in which to accept the offer of legal aid, otherwise the offer may lapse, resulting in you having to reapply.

Costs and damages

If you are in receipt of legal aid, the Legal Aid Board may recover any costs and general damages awarded to you as a result of court proceedings or a settlement reached out of court. The board will be entitled to deduct the costs it has incurred from any monies that you receive, subject to a few limited exceptions. As soon as possible after the conclusion of your case, either through court proceedings or via an agreed settlement, the Legal Aid Board will furnish you with a statement setting out:

~ A summary of the legal services provided.

~ The total amount of any general damages, costs or any other monies recovered by or preserved for you and lodged to the fund.

~ A breakdown of the costs incurred by the board on your behalf in providing legal services.

A final thought

Whether or not you qualify to receive legal aid, or choose to take it up if you do, it is an option worth considering. You may have concerns that the level of advice or representation will be in some way inferior if you take the legal aid route, but you can rest assured that it is in fact as good as any legal service available on the open market.

The forms for applying for legal aid are in the Appendix on page 187.

Legal Aid Board addresses

Head office

The address for the head office of the Legal Aid Board is Quay Street, Cahirciveen, County Kerry, and they can be contacted on (066) 9471000. The Dublin office is based at Montague Court, Montague Street, Dublin 2, and can be contacted on (01) 4776200.

Cavan
Newcourt Shopping Centre, Church Street, County Cavan
Tel: (049) 4331110
Fax: (049) 4331304

Clare
Unit 6a, Merchant's Square, Ennis, County Clare
Tel: (065) 6821929
Fax: (065) 6821939

Cork
North Quay House, Popes Quay, Cork
Tel: (021) 4551686
Fax: (021) 4551690

1a South Mall, Cork
Tel: (021) 4275998
Fax: (021) 4276927

Donegal
Houston House, Main Street, Letterkenny, County Donegal
Tel: (074) 9126177
Fax: (074) 9126086

Dublin
45 Lower Gardiner Street, Dublin 1
Tel: (01) 8745440

9 Lower Ormond Quay, Dublin 1
Tel: (01) 8724133

Tower Centre, Clondalkin Village, Dublin 22
Tel: (01) 4576011

44/49 Main Street, Finglas, Dublin 11
Tel: (01) 8640314

Unit 6–8, Business Centre, Clonsilla Road, Blanchardstown, Dublin 15
Tel: (01) 8200455

Village Green, Tallaght, Dublin 24
Tel: (01) 4511519

48/49 North Brunswick Street, Georges Lane, Dublin 7
Tel: (01) 6469700

Galway
9 St Francis Street, Galway
Tel: (091) 561650

Kerry
1 Day Place, Tralee, County Kerry
Tel: (066) 7126900

Kildare
Canning Place, Newbridge, County Kildare
Tel: (045) 435777

Kilkenny
86 Maudlin Street, Kilkenny
Tel: (056) 7761611

Laois
Unit 6a, Bridge Street, Portlaoise, County Laois
Tel: (0502) 61366

Limerick
Lock Quay, Limerick
Tel: (061) 314599

Longford
Credit Union Courtyard, 50a Main Street, Longford
Tel: (043) 47590

Louth
Roden Place, Dundalk, County Louth
Tel: (042) 930448

Mayo
Humbert Mall, Main Street, Castlebar, County Mayo
Tel: (094) 9024334

Meath
Kennedy Road, Navan, County Meath
Tel: (046) 9072515

Monaghan
Alma House, The Diamond, Monaghan
Tel: (04) 84888

Offaly
Harbour Street, Tullamore, County Offaly
Tel: (0506) 51177

Sligo
Bridgewater House, Rockwood Parade, Thomas Street, Sligo
Tel: (071) 9161670

Tipperary
Friarscourt, Nenagh, County Tipperary
Tel: (067) 34181

Waterford
Canada House, Canada Street, Waterford
Tel: (051) 855814

Westmeath
Northgate Street, Athlone, County Westmeath
Tel: (09064) 74694

Wexford
Unit 8, Redmond Square, Wexford
Tel: (053) 22622

Wicklow
Bridge Street, Wicklow
Tel: (0404) 66166

Part-time centres

St Catherine's Social Services Centre, St Joseph's Road, County Carlow
Tel: (0503) 31354

Kilrush Community Centre, Toler Street, Kilrush, County Clare
Tel: (065) 6821929

The Courthouse, Donegal Town, County Donegal
Tel: (074) 926177

Killarney Community Services Centre, 57 High Street, Killarney, County Kerry
Tel: (066) 7126900

North Western Health Board, Leitrim Road, Carrick-on-Shannon, County Leitrim
Tel: (043) 47590

Drogheda Community Services Centre, Fair Street, Drogheda, County Louth
Tel: (041) 36084/33490

Ballina Community Centre, Teeling Street, Ballina, County Mayo
Tel: (096) 24334

Health Centre, Knock Road, Ballyhaunis, County Mayo
Tel: (091) 561650

Citizens' information Centre, Patrick's Street, County Roscommon
Tel: (071) 961670

Thurles Community Social Services, Rossa Street, Thurles, County Tipperary
Tel: (067) 34181

Citizens' Information Centre, 14 Wellington Street, Clonmel, County Tipperary
Tel: (052) 22267

Enterprise Centre, Bishopgate Street, Mullingar, County Westmeath
Tel: (0902) 74694

[6]

HOW THE COURTS WORK

We have all seen Ally McBeal strutting her stuff on the courtroom floor with Al Greene in the background, or *Law and Order*, where hard-hitting lawyers win massive awards for their clients against the odds. Some of us may also have memories of *Crown Court* and all those white wigs. Well, the family court in Ireland is nothing like any of these. In fact, it is about as far removed as you can get.

The court processes are dealt with in subsequent chapters, but here we will set the stage and look at a few basic facts about the family courts in Ireland.

Your privacy

Many people fear that going to court is like washing their dirty linen in public, that their private affairs will be made known to other people and become fodder for gossip. However, in family law this will not happen. All family law cases in Ireland are currently heard in private. No member of the general public is allowed to be present in the courtroom, not even a family member for support. This is called the in-camera rule ('in-camera' means in private). The Civil Liability and Courts Bill (2004) may have some effect on the in-camera rule if it passed into law. This is discussed further in the 'in-camera rule' section on page 76. The only people who are allowed to be present in the courtroom during a family law hearing are the following:

~ The judge

~ The judge's crier

~ The applicant

~ The respondent

~ Solicitors for both sides

~ Barristers for both sides

~ The court registrar (This is the person who notes the details of the order of the court and any other relevant points. The 'order of the court' is the decision the judge announces when the hearing is over. The court registrar will also note any other relevant details, such as a possible date for a further hearing, etc. These notes are for court use only, and are not available to any member of the public.)

~ A court stenographer (who, in some cases, can be hired by either side to take shorthand notes of what is said during the court hearing and of any order of the court)

~ Any other court administration staff the judge requires

~ Anyone required to give testimony during your case (for example, court-appointed psychologist who may have prepared a report in relation to issues in your case,

such as access, etc.) can attend the court
for the purpose of giving testimony.
However, they are only allowed to enter
the courtroom when called to give their
testimony, and must leave once they have
finished. They are not allowed to remain
in the courtroom while the rest of your
case is being heard.

If the family hearing is also to resolve issues in relation to
any children of the marriage, those children are not
allowed to be present during the course of the hearing.

The in-camera rule

At the time that I was seeking a judicial separation
through the Irish court system, a rule known as the in-
camera rule was in operation. The effect of this rule was
to afford both parties privacy at a very stressful time. It
did so by ensuring that the courtrooms where family law
cases are heard were sealed. This meant that only the
relevant parties involved in the case (see 'Your privacy'
section, page 73) were allowed in the courtroom during
the hearing of the case.

While appreciative of the privacy this afforded me,
allowing my case to be brought to a conclusion in a very
private way, there was one way in which it did in fact add
to the stress of the whole situation. The absence of family
law case reports meant that you were solely reliant on
your legal team to advise you on the possible outcome of
your case.

I fully understand that family law was and is by no
means an exact science, in the sense that the courts did
not hand out standardised decisions. To do so could, as

with mandatory sentences in criminal law, lead to harsh and ultimately unjust outcomes. Each case was dealt with on its own merits and the courts had a wide range of options in relation to the outcome. While discretion in the court's decision is clearly an important element in family law cases, as is the protection of the parties' identities, the lack of reports left myself and others very much in the dark as to the type of decisions made in family law.

Another downside to the in-camera rule as I experienced it during my separation process applied if a problem arose with one's solicitor or legal team. If this was the case, there was not a lot you could do, because the in-camera rule prohibited reporting to anyone what had occurred in the family law proceedings. This meant that it was impossible to bring a complaint to the Bar Council (in the case of barristers) or the Law Society (in the case of solicitors) if you believed you had cause for complaint.

In July 2004 the Civil Liability and Courts Bill (2004) was brought to the Seanad. This could have huge significance for family law cases in Ireland, not only because of the changes it may herald but also because it is, in my mind, one of the first acknowledgments of the need to modernise the treatment of family law in the courts in Ireland. Although the Bill has yet to be passed, my research indicates that it will bring about some major changes. As I understand it, the issues under discussion are:

~ The media may now be allowed access to the family law courts in order to report on the outcome of cases. However, they may only report on the decisions of the court in relation to family law. They will not be in a position to reveal any information which could lead to the identification of any parties to the proceedings. In this way, for the first time it may be possible for the decisions of the family law courts to be reported on, while still affording protection by way of privacy to the parties involved.

~ Currently, the parties identified in the section 'Your privacy' (see page 74) are the only parties allowed to be present in the courtroom. While this can be very stressful for most, it is particularly stressful for those applicants or respondents who have been victims of domestic violence at the hands of their estranged spouse. Now, for the first time it may be possible to have someone accompany you in the courtroom for moral support. The application of this rule, if it is passed, will be at the discretion of the judge hearing your case.

~ Given the possible relaxation of the in-camera rule, it may now also become possible to bring a complaint in relation to your legal team to the relevant governing body, the Bar Council (in the case of barristers) and the Law Society (in the case of solicitors).

These are some of the possible changes the Bill will herald if it is passed into law. Whether or not this happens, it would appear to me that, given the constant media debate in relation to family law and the pressure that is being brought by those who have been through the process, it will inevitably bring about changes in the way family law cases are heard, which I believe will be to the benefit of all involved. Even if the above or indeed other changes are made it may not be possible for some time to assess their success, as the potential gap between implementation and assessment is as yet an unknown variable. Either way, it would seem that sooner or later the winds of change will inevitably blow.

What is the courtroom like?

The judge is usually dressed in business attire, not a wig and gown. Your barrister will not wear a wig and gown either. This makes the court seem less daunting and less formal than other courtrooms. You will sit at the back of the room, as will your estranged spouse, but there will be space between the two of you. Your barrister will be at a table in front of you with his/her back turned to you, facing the judge. Your solicitor will sit at the opposite side of the table to the barrister, facing you. Behind your legal team and in front of the judge is where the court registrar normally sits, taking notes and passing any relevant paperwork back and forth between the barristers and the judge. The judge sits at the top of the room on what can best be described as a raised podium.

What are the courts like?

Courts are not the most luxurious of places. Each court usually has a couple of courtrooms both running their own list of cases or motions for the day. Yours will probably not be the only case or motion being heard on the day you are in court. If the court is not a designated family law court, as in Dublin, there may be other cases outside of family law being heard, although the court should still be sealed for all family law matters (see page 75 for discussion of the in-camera rule). The types of case being heard, whether full separation hearings or just motions for more minor family-related issues, will affect how many people will be around on the day. Courts are usually busy places, with numerous solicitors, barristers, clerks and registrars, as well as the parties whose cases are going to be heard and sometimes even their friends or family, brought along for moral support. In some cases, expert witnesses and other witnesses may also be present and generally have to be there from when the court opens.

There are no canteen facilities or luxurious waiting-rooms. There may be a limited number of small meeting-rooms which can be used free of charge, on a first-come-first-served basis, by you and your legal team to discuss your case with a degree of privacy. If these rooms are all taken, you will have to wait in the corridor or waiting area. This can mean that you end up trying to find a quiet corner to speak with your legal team, often in full view of your estranged spouse and his/her legal team.

My intention is not to fill you with despair, but it is better to be prepared for the reality of the situation you may have to deal with on the day. If the thought of going to court causes you a great deal of stress, you should try to call in, even if only for five minutes, on a day before your own case comes up. If you are at least a bit familiar with the court, it will be one less thing to worry about on the day.

Will I be given a time for my case to be heard?

I found that the court doors usually opened at around 9 a.m. Sometimes queues had started forming outside the court by 8.30 a.m. as people tried to ensure they got a meeting-room. No case is heard before 10.30 a.m. When the judge for the courtroom where your case will be heard arrives, he will hold a call-over at about 10.30 a.m. This is when the judge meets with all the solicitors and barristers who have clients appearing in court that day. You will not need to be present. The judge will ask each legal team if they have the relevant parties present (i.e. you and your estranged spouse) and if you are ready to proceed. The judge will then decide the order in which those who are ready will be heard. Call-over is also the time when the judge will be made aware of those who wish to adjourn their case, for whatever reason. It may be that someone is sick or they may simply not have shown up, in which case the judge decides whether or not the case can go ahead and, if not, the date to which it will be reassigned.

There is no set time for each case, but your legal team will have indicated to the court the probable time needed when applying for a hearing date. You will hear the court registrar call out the first case. The length of time it takes will depend on the kind of case it is. Most judges will try to hear the shorter cases first and leave those that may take more time to the end of the day.

This means that there may be a lot of waiting around before your case is called. Bear in mind too that different courts may vary in their approach to scheduling.

What if there is not enough time?

If the case prior to yours runs over the projected time, there may not be enough time to hear your case. In this eventuality, it will be adjourned to another day. While this is very frustrating, it is something which does sometimes happen, so you should be prepared for that possibility. The longer the projected time needed for your case, the greater the possibility that it will be adjourned, as it is likely to be at the end of the court list. In some instances, when a case has started but has not finished by the close of business that day, the balance of the case will be held over to another day. Obviously, it is preferable for the case to continue the following day, but it can happen that several days, and in some cases even weeks or months, can pass before the end of the hearing. While everything will be done to avoid this, you should be aware that it can happen. If your case is spread over more than one day, it will be heard by the same judge.

Specially fixed date

If your case keeps being adjourned, an application can be made by either side to have a 'specially fixed date'. This is where a date is assigned for your case, which may be the only case heard on that particular day. All applications for a case, even if not on a specifically fixed date, must be accompanied by a letter certifying that all the relevant information for the court to make a decision about your case will be available to the court and discovery has been complied with in full on both sides. This information may include fully vouched valuations, affidavits of means, notices to trustees, statements of benefits, and any expert reports that are required. A realistic estimate of the duration of the hearing should also be given.

Will I have to testify?

There are two main ways a judge can make a decision in relation to your case, either by means of written evidence or by presenting oral evidence. All the relevant information can be given by means of a sworn affidavit. A sworn affidavit is a legal document, which is your statement outlining the reliefs you are looking for and why you are looking for them. Where there is an interim issue to be resolved (such as interim maintenance payments or access and custody) before the final hearing, such motions are usually dealt with on the basis of affidavits, although the judge may sometimes decide to hear oral evidence from both parties. The barristers on both sides are free to speak or argue the case, based on the information given in the affidavits. The applicant's barrister usually speaks first, followed by the respondent's barrister. The judge may ask questions to clarify any queries s/he may have. In some cases, your barrister may lean across to ask you to clarify something and will then confirm that detail with the judge. However, in this situation, as all evidence is given in written form, you will not be required to testify.

At the final hearing of the case, the evidence required will be oral. You will be asked to step into the witness box – which may just be a chair alongside the judge – where you will have to take an oath swearing to tell the truth. You will be asked questions by your own barrister first, followed by questions from the barrister for the other side – the respondent. Most questions will be confined to the facts outlined in both affidavits. Your barrister will be given the opportunity to re-examine you to clarify any points which have been brought up by the opposing side.

Who testifies first?

The person who has applied to have the case heard and is seeking the relief against the opposing party is the applicant. Given that the applicant is seeking the relief, s/he is the first to testify. The respondent testifies after the applicant has been questioned by both sides. When either the applicant or the respondent is testifying, their own legal team will question them first.

If you do have to testify

It is hard to be in court dealing with issues that are often very emotional and feeling under pressure from someone you used to share your life with. It is a stressful situation to find yourself in, so here are some pointers to help you get through.

~ Just answer the question you are asked; don't stray from the point.

~ In some cases, a 'yes' or 'no' is sufficient. It is not a case of quantity but of facts.

~ Speak clearly and slowly, so that the judge can hear you and to avoid ambiguity.

~ If you do not understand the question, say so.

~ If you do not know the answer, say so.

~ Do not get personal or turn the proceedings into a slanging match. Remember, judges hear case after case, day after day, week after week, and there is probably not a lot you can say that they have not heard before. The judge will just be concerned with the facts of the case, not that your ex-spouse was hard to live with, etc. Such remarks are not usually relevant and will only confuse the hearing of your case.

~ Try to remain as objective as possible. Remember why you are there and what you hope to achieve. A cheap jibe at the expense of your estranged spouse will not help you achieve that and may just muddy the waters.

~ If you get flustered, or need a drink of water, or are finding it very stressful – just say so.

~ Stay focused.

~ Try to relax and take your time answering. Your barrister will ask questions that are designed to help you, giving you the opportunity to have your case heard and get the most relevant points across to the judge. Focus on this and see it as your chance to present your case in a positive way.

Everyone who has to give evidence in a courtroom will be nervous. That is perfectly normal. Do not feel under pressure to perform or be too over-enthusiastic with your answers. Judges always operate under the same parameters and with the same objectives. Some of the things you want to say may not be relevant, so try not to cloud the issues.

Consulting with your solicitor or barrister

You will not be allowed to consult with your solicitor or barrister about your case until you have finished giving your evidence. If, when you are giving evidence the court takes a break for lunch or to return the next day, your barrister and solicitor are legally bound not to enter into any discussion of your case with you until all your evidence is given. So if you find yourself in a situation where the court breaks for lunch halfway through your testimony, do not be worried if your legal representatives do not discuss the case with you – they can't.

Court opening hours

A day in court is not the full nine-to-five day you may expect. The court only opens for case hearings at about 10.30 a.m. This is followed by the call-over (as explained earlier) and the first case will start shortly after 10.30 a.m. The court will then run until around 1.00 p.m., when it breaks for lunch. Court reconvenes after lunch at 2 p.m. and ends at 4 p.m., or sometimes 4.30 p.m. in order to finish hearing the end of a case.

Courts do not run for a full fifty-two weeks a year, as they close for various holiday periods throughout the course of the year. An example of opening times can be seen if we look at the timetable of the opening times for a previous year, where the court was open from 13 January to 11 April, when it closed for the Easter break. It reopened on 28 April and remained open until 5 June, when it closed until 18 June. From then it was open until 31 July, at which point it closed for the summer period and did not reopen until 6 October. It then ran until 19

December, when it closed for the Christmas break. Each year's schedule depends on when the natural breaks, like Easter and Christmas, fall.

Applying for a court date

Do not be surprised if you apply for a court date and it is not possible to get one for several months. The waiting list can be long, which is why it is important for your solicitor to run to schedule in the processing of paperwork in order to get your case listed as soon as possible. If your case requires an interim application (known as a motion), such as an urgent application for maintenance or access, it should be possible to get a date sooner rather than later. The courts are well used to receiving applications for hearings which need to be listed before the court term ends and the court clerks will try to facilitate this. Although the court does not sit during vacation periods, it may be possible to bring an urgent interim application to the court during these periods. Usually such applications will be of an important nature.

Once the court process starts, is it too late to settle amicably?

A judge sitting in the family law court would much prefer it if both sides could reach an amicable settlement with each other. The legislation also encourages both parties to settle their case if possible. If the case has started and one or other side wishes to make an offer of settlement to the other, they can still do so. You will have to decide whether or not you want to settle, or make a counter offer, or return to court to have the rest of your case heard. The judge will not be aware of the content of any discussions or offers between the sides. The decision is yours. If, during the course of your hearing, or prior to your hearing on the day, a settlement can be reached, your case will not be heard and can be cancelled at the last minute.

Settlement meetings prior to a hearing

A settlement meeting can be requested by either side prior to the hearing. If one side requests it, the other side is not obliged to attend and can wait to go to court. My advice would be to attend. If there is any chance of reaching your own solution, you should at least consider it. Settlement meetings are par for the course prior to a court case (see the section 'Settlement meetings' in Chapter 3, page 40).

Is a decision made at a settlement meeting legally binding?

If you are fortunate enough to be able to reach a solution without having your case heard, your legal team will draw up the terms of the agreement between the two of you. This is then signed by both the husband and wife. Once approved by both sides, this agreement will be submitted to the court and the court will make the terms of such an agreement an order of the court. This has the effect of making such a mutually agreed settlement legally binding and, if it is subsequently reneged on, you can seek the remedies of the court.

If you can reach agreement on some, but not all, of the issues that need to be sorted out, these can be taken off the table, and you can go to court to resolve the issues you cannot agree on. The court will still make the items you agreed on part of the final court order – your barrister will present them, the other side will agree and the judge will so order.

Will I be told the court's order on the same day as my case?

It is not unusual for the judge to announce his/her decision on the day that the case is heard. If, however, the issues in your case are quite substantive and a large amount of evidence has been heard or the case has been heard over a number of days, the judge may require some time to consider all the facts presented to the court and may schedule another day for you to come back and hear the court's decision. This is known as reserving judgment. This may mean that a number of weeks will elapse between your case finishing and the order being made known. The court will usually give a date for the delivery of the judgment at the end of the hearing, and on that day you will hear the judge deliver the written judgment and order.

How will I be able to prove what the court ordered?

Once a court makes a final order in relation to the issues of your case, the court clerk will make notes of the judgment as ruled on by the court. All these points will then be put into writing in a document known as an order of the court. The document will contain both the applicant's and the respondent's name, the record number of your case and the details of the award made by the court. It will be stamped by the court and, when it is ready, the solicitors for each side will be able to take a copy and forward it on to you. The only parties entitled to a copy of the order are both the parties involved, the legal representatives for each side and anyone else that the court orders should receive a copy. If a solicitor is on record for you (i.e. representing you), s/he is the one entitled to take up copy order, not you directly. No other private individual will be able to go to the courts and have sight of, or receive a copy of, the order.

Will I be able to get a copy of the order on the day I appear in court?

Except in very exceptional circumstances, the court clerk will not have a copy of the order ready on the same day as the judge delivers the ruling of the court in relation to your case. During the period when I was going through the process of legal separation, the time that elapsed between being in court, hearing the order and actually receiving the order was sometimes several months. However, depending on where the judgment is given, the procedure is now different. In Dublin, the circuit court registrar engrosses (i.e. signs) the order. Outside of Dublin, a draft (agreed by the solicitors) is submitted to the county registrar, who signs it if s/he approves it or sends it back with changes. Once these changes are incorporated, it is then resubmitted for signing. This has speeded up the process considerably.

[7]

WHAT THE COURTS CAN MAKE JUDGMENTS ON

This has to be one of the scariest parts. A stranger will make a decision that will affect you for the rest of your life. But remember what I said at the beginning: if you end up in court it should be because you had no other option, so whatever you come out with is better than what you would have had if you had let things be. Also, not everything has to come under the hammer. If there is an issue on which you and you estranged spouse can agree, this does not have to be part of the court's decision-making process but can be incorporated into the order once both parties reach agreement on it. Indeed, even during the course of your court case, if you and your spouse can reach agreement on even some aspects relating to your separation, they will be taken off the judge's table for decision but can be incorporated as part of the overall court order.

Orders of the court

When a court (the judge) makes a decision in relation to the outcome of your case, it is called an order. This order is then put into writing and stamped with the official seal of the court. It is legally binding on both sides. A copy of the court order can be obtained from the court clerk by either of the parties involved (if acting lay litigant) or by their solicitors after the judgment is made. You are bound by the order of the court for as long as the order is in place. For example, an order may be in place until the children of the marriage reach the age of eighteen and then it expires. The court may also make an order in relation to money or other financial aspects for a specific period of time. It depends on all the variables of your case.

Most importantly, courts take the orders that they make very seriously. They will view someone who breaks such an order in a very poor light. Even if there are mitigating circumstances for breaking the order, a court will normally still take the view that you are bound by the order while it is still in existence and has not been varied.

However, you should not feel too alarmed. A court will give you leave to apply to vary the decision or part of it at a later date if circumstances have changed. The most common applications to vary an order are usually made in connection with ongoing maintenance and access rights. There is no guarantee that the court will vary the order and, even if they do, they may not vary it according to your wishes. However, you do have leave to apply.

The orders the court can make are wide and varied, and not every case will require all the remedies that can be offered by the court. The following are the usual orders a court makes judgments on in relation to family law proceedings:

~ Custody and guardianship
~ Access to children
~ Ownership of the family home
~ Occupation of the family home
~ Division of other property and assets (shares, savings accounts, etc.)
~ Orders in relation to pension rights for either party
~ Succession rights
~ Maintenance
~ Lump sum payments
~ Passports for children
~ Birthing costs
~ Barring and safety orders

The courts also have the right to make orders to help them make decisions or facilitate any of the above orders.

Before you apply for any of the above reliefs in a court, you should make yourself aware of some of the possible outcomes and the limits the courts will apply to making orders. There is nothing worse then being ill-prepared for a possible decision of the court and finding yourself bound by an order that you were not even aware could be made. Make sure you know everything that a court is being asked to make a decision on by either side.

While you may be advised of the possible options and of what you should look for, remember one thing: no one will know your case as well as you. As important as it is to get good legal advice, and to really 'hear' the advice you are given, it is equally important to consider options which you are really happy with. Here we will briefly run through each of the above areas to give you an idea of what they are about.

Custody and guardianship

As you read the word 'custody', you can probably feel yourself getting hot under the collar. I deliberately start with this one, as it is one of the orders that can evoke the most emotional responses and become one of the biggest bones of contention. People often confuse the meaning of the word 'custody' with the meaning of the word 'guardianship'. So let us start with guardianship.

Guardianship is an automatic legal right granted to both the mother and father of a child once that child has been born to both in marriage. This right is something a court is unlikely to remove from either parent, except in extremely unusual circumstances. In a nutshell, guardians are entitled to make decisions regarding things such as the education of the child, the religion the child will be raised in and all decisions relating to the overall care and welfare of the child, ranging from crèches, schools, doctors, medical care, etc. All such decisions should be made in consultation with the other guardian. In the event of the custodial spouse (i.e. the spouse with whom the child or children reside) dying, then custody of the children automatically passes to the other guardian/parent.

Custody, on the other hand, refers to where the child actually lives and who the child resides with on a full-time basis. The other guardian/parent is usually granted access rights. In the majority of cases, custody (i.e. the day-to-day care and control of the children) is granted to the mother of the child and access rights are granted to the father. This means that set times are laid down during which the non-custodial parent has the right to spend time with the child or children.

Many people talk about fighting for custody rights. However, they often do not realise that the rights of guardianship which you already have in this situation can outweigh the custody rights. The word 'custody' should not be confused with having the right to have a say in your child's life – you already have that. The reality is that, in a lot of cases, the children of a marriage end up residing with the mother after a separation, and this constitutes custody. The custodial parent is under an obligation, however, to keep the other parent (the one with access rights) fully informed about all aspects of the child's life and consult the other person about all decisions in connection with the life of the child. The fact that a child or children live with the custodial parent should not in any way limit the rights and duties of the other guardian; it just limits the amount of time the guardian seeking access spends with them.

Access

Access is dealt with in Chapter 11.

The family home

I presumed the family home was where I lived with my spouse, and that was in fact about right, but there were many other things surrounding this area that I was not aware of when I started out, so let me address some of the questions I had at the beginning of my journey.

What is the family home?
The family home is where two people who are married normally reside. It is the primary residential address for both people. That's about it in a nutshell.

What if one person owned the family home prior to getting married?

Even if one spouse lived in and owned the home prior to marriage, it automatically becomes the family home once both spouses live there as a married couple. This can have a number of effects.

- Even if only one spouse is named on the deeds of the house, once it becomes the marital home the spouse named on the deeds cannot sell, transfer or re-mortgage the family home without the written consent of the other spouse.

- Prior to a formal judicial separation or separation agreement, when the spouses are informally separated, both parties are still entitled to have access to the family home. One party cannot suddenly change the locks and refuse the other party entry.

- Post judicial separation, even if the house remains in the ownership of the non-custodial parent, the court can make an order excluding that person from the family home for life or such shorter period as the court decides.

- Before taking any form of legal route, many couples who have separated may stay living under the same roof. Given today's rental market and increased living costs, it may not be feasible for one party to move out. Added to this, both parties may feel uncomfortable about leaving the family home.

How will the court decide who, if anyone, gets to remain in the family home?

When going to court to sort out your issues in relation to a separation, one of the things your solicitor will seek is an order in relation to the family home. This order is known as a property adjustment order, and is where one or both parties seek to have a decision made in relation to either the sale, occupation or ownership of the family home. The court can make a number of different kinds of orders in relation to the family home and your solicitor and or barrister should make you aware of them all and what in their opinion is most likely to happen. If you have a specific idea as to what you want the decision about the family home to be, even if it differs from the options that have been suggested to you, make sure your solicitor and barrister are aware of it. They will let you know whether in their opinion you should proceed with making that particular application.

Some of the possible orders a court can make in relation to the family home

The court can order that the custodial guardian of the children has a right to remain living in the family home until the youngest child reaches the age of eighteen. If the youngest child goes into further education after leaving school, the court may decide to allow them to reside in the family home until the child reaches the age of twenty-three, when their education is complete.

This road may be fraught with problems, for a number of reasons, let alone those that may arise further down the road. Although a court cannot make an order based on what you think may or may not happen in the future, it is something you should think about and which should have some degree of influence on the decisions you make now. Consider the following scenarios.

If, when a couple separate, their youngest child is in his/her middle to late teens, it seems reasonable to leave them living in their family home, as causing disruption at that point will be very upsetting for the child/children. To wait a couple of years, at which point the house will probably be sold, will not put either party out as much as if the order were to cover a period greater than five years – say fifteen or sixteen.

My own belief is that separating is a painful enough process, and it makes sense to try to resolve all of the issues as quickly as possible and not drag them out. The age of your children may have a direct impact on what your housing requirements are, so bear this in mind too. For both parties, the issue of ownership of the family home can be very unsettling. It also opens up other complications that may need to be addressed further down the line. Addressing ownership of the family home is an important issue. It is worth considering the following scenarios if ownership has not been addressed:

- ∿ The ex-spouse moves out, then marries another party and subsequently dies. Would the second wife have a potential claim on your home as part of her late husband's estate?

- ∿ If your ex-spouse has other children and is still an owner of the family home, would your rights be affected?

- ∿ What if the spouse residing in the home remarries or chooses to live with his or her new partner in the family home?

- ∿ What if the partner residing in the family home has children with his/her new partner and that relationship subsequently also ends?

~ If you are left in a position where you have to find a new home a decade down the road, and if you need additional finance to help you purchase that home, you may have difficulty getting a loan, due to the shorter payback time you have prior to retirement.

~ No one could have predicted the house price increases over the last few years, so who can make provision for what they may be in the future. To leave such a major factor in your life undecided for many years to come could be a source of considerable stress in the future.

~ As you get older, there is an increased possibility of health problems or other factors entering the arena. Would it not be better to sort out the issue of housing at a point in time when it is possible to do so, rather than putting it off until the distant future?

I do not raise the above issues from a legal perspective but with a view to pointing out the personal choices you may have to make in the future. Leaving some issues unresolved, particularly ones as important as the family home, can cause many emotional problems further down the line. If there is more than one issue unresolved, they are likely to spill over into each other.

A court can order that the family home be sold and the proceeds, after the costs and solicitor's fees have been deducted, split between the two parties. This can mean a fifty-fifty split, but not always. A court is free to decide what percentage of the profits (assuming there is a profit) each party is entitled to receive, based on the particular facts of your case which have been presented to the court.

A court can order the delay of the sale of the family

home, possibly in order to let the residing party find new accommodation, or for whatever reason it sees fit.

A court can award the house to one party and order that the ownership be transferred into the sole name of the party to whom it has been awarded. The court could also make additional orders; for example, that the party who has been awarded the home pays a sum of money to the party whose name is being removed from the deeds.

Given the costs of buying a home in Ireland today, it would usually take two salaries combined to get a mortgage. If both people are taking the loan, it will probably be a stipulation of the terms of the loan from the lending institution that both parties' names are on the deeds. If the deeds of the home are in the sole name of just one of the parties, the court can order the transfer of the family home into joint names. A court may make a decision about the family home in combination with a decision about other assets of the marriage. For example, if a couple were residing in the family home but had other property interests together, a court may award one party the family home and the other party part or all of the other property interests. Each party would usually then sign away their rights to the other property thus awarded.

Division of other property and assets

No matter what the list of assets, the courts are only interested in making decisions in relation to substantive ones. Aside from the family home, these would include any other property or land, bank accounts, shares, savings schemes, including anything that is held in joint names or has a financial implication for either or both parties. This could also include such things as valuable paintings, family heirlooms, etc., where the emotional attachment may in some cases outweigh the financial ones. The court will not get involved in which party gets which CD, or book, or piece of crockery (not that they couldn't make an order if they so decided, as technically these items are still marital property), so don't waste its time. No solicitor or barrister is going to want to seek a decision on the beer mat collection.

Orders in relation to the pension rights of either party

At a point where I still had a good thirty years of employment ahead of me, the idea of arguing over future potential pension rights never even entered my head. However, even though, for me, it did not seem very relevant, for many it is and should be. This is especially true if one party has been the home-maker and the other has had a pension plan in place during his/her working career, which could be quite a valuable asset if that person has been working for any length of time. I refer to it as an asset, as I was informed at the time of my own separation that it was indeed viewed by the court as an asset and one that a decision has to be reached on. Often the pension is the second most valuable asset after the family home.

A person wishing to make a claim on a pension would seek what is known as a 'pension adjustment order'. I explored this area, more out of curiosity as to what such an order could cover, and, as with the family home, found the court could make quite a range of orders.

~ A court can order that part of the pension of the working spouse be paid to the other spouse.

~ It can order that part of the pension of the working spouse is paid to a dependent child.

∼ If the other spouse is in, or returning to the workforce, the court can order that part of one spouse's pension be split and placed in the pension fund of the other person. The percentage of the split will be decided by the court.

∼ The court can also make a decision on death in service benefit; for instance, that the spouse is still the spouse for the purpose of this benefit.

The type of order a court will make in relation to a pension will depend on the type of pension held by either party. You should make sure you are familiar with the terms of both your pension (if you have one) and your spouse's (if they have one). Types of pensions and the contributions to them can differ from company to company. Also, some people may not have a company pension scheme but will be contributing to a pension scheme outside the remit of their employer, a private pension.

Succession rights

I remember hearing my solicitor talk about succession rights early on in my case. I did not really listen, as I was too busy thinking about the here and now – about the bills I had to pay this month – to think about something so far down the line. Put simply, succession rights refer to each spouse's right to claim against the other's property if they were to die. 'Property' here means the assets of their estate, not just the house they live in.

As part of a judicial separation, the court decides if the succession rights of one or both parties are to be extinguished. This does not negate any child or children's right to claim against the estate of their parent – you cannot sign away your child's succession rights, just your own.

A court will not usually extinguish the succession rights of a spouse unless that spouse is adequately provided for. In today's world where many spouses are both working full time, both parties may be required to sign away their succession rights against the other spouse.

While this may not seem very important, the freedom it affords you is that you are free to make a will and bequeath your assets in whatever manner you see fit. Your ex-spouse, if s/he survives you, will not be able to make a claim against your estate and thus impact on the content of your will.

When you are married, even if you draft a will, the law clearly provides for your spouse's legal right to claim against your estate and makes provision for the percentage of the estate to which they may be legally entitled. A spouse cannot draft a will which removes this legal right from you. However, once you are divorced, and therefore no longer legally married, succession rights usually are no longer relevant and you have no legal claim against each other's estate.

If a spouse who is paying maintenance dies, you should, however, be able to make a claim against their estate for money owing to you in relation to the maintenance of any children of the marriage.

Once you have obtained a judicial separation, you should consult with your solicitor about the possibility or need for drafting a will.

Maintenance

See Chapter 10.

Lump sum payments

When trying to reach a solution regarding my own case, I decided that I wanted a solution that brought about closure on as many issues as possible. The idea of having ongoing issues for years to come held no appeal for me. Many people talk about trying to reach a place where they have closure, but this can mean different things to different people. For me, closure meant finding a way to move on with my own life, a way of making my own decisions independently of anyone else. Obviously, when it comes to children, all parental decisions have to be made jointly, but I felt it was important to avoid having ongoing court orders which could see me back in court year after year.

One way of limiting the contact with an ex-spouse and all the possible pain that it can entail is to try to reduce the number of ongoing court orders between both parties and to get as many finite decisions in relation to orders as possible. If the relationship is particularly acrimonious between both parties, lump sum payments may be one way of reducing future friction. A lump sum payment circumvents, at least for a period of time, having to deal with ongoing orders on a weekly or monthly basis which can be used by either party against the other. It will also prevent any possible breaches of maintenance orders for the period the lump sum payment covers, as, by its nature, payment is received in advance. This means that no arguments about maintenance are likely to ensue for the period the lump sum covers.

A 'lump sum order' is an order instructing one spouse to pay the other a lump sum of money instead of having to pay periodic payments. This does not negate one party's liability to pay maintenance to the other party, either in respect of the spouse or of the children, but it provides for a maintenance payment up front. Lump sum payments can sometimes be ordered in addition to periodic maintenance payments.

Obviously, a decision about this depends on the circumstances of both parties and whether or not it is financially practical for such an order to be put in place. If an order will cause undue financial hardship on the party paying the amount, it is unlikely to be considered by the court, in which case it is unlikely that you will be advised to seek one. If, however, the other party is in a financial position that makes such a payment possible, it may be considered by the court.

I think this kind of payment has benefits for both sides. The person paying, while taking an initial financial hit, will have the freedom to make financial decisions without having to consider an ongoing weekly/monthly award. If that party subsequently wishes to change career, start a business of his/her own, or take time out, s/he will be free to do so. If that spouse is seeking a business loan or a new mortgage, s/he will have more disposable income with which to make future plans. The party in receipt of the maintenance will be able to make plans for the future and maintain a lifestyle for which they can plan accordingly.

The circumstances of your case will dictate whether or not this is something which can be considered by the courts – but it may prove a better solution for both parties involved.

The lump sum payment that can be awarded depends on which court the application is made to. The district court has a cap that it will not award a lump sum in excess of €6,348.69. You should check at the time of your application what level is currently in place, as this may change. You can do so by calling your local court office.

Passports for children

When access orders are put in place, one item that may come up for mention is passports for the children. A passport will usually be granted to the child or children to be held by the custodial parent. It is becoming more and more common for children to be issued with their own passport instead of being included on one parent's passport. There will be set conditions regarding taking the children on holiday. Normally, if this is an issue in court, the judge will make various orders in relation to taking the children abroad. These could include the following.

- ∼ The children will often not be allowed to be taken to a non-Hague Convention country.
- ∼ The other parent must be given full details of where the children are going on holiday.
- ∼ The children may not be taken out of the country for more than three weeks, for example, unless with the other parent's consent.
- ∼ The parent not accompanying the children must be given adequate notice of the holiday.

Birthing costs

Giving birth can be an expensive business, between medical costs and baby equipment. Both parents have a responsibility to maintain their children, and both have a responsibility to meet the birthing costs for bringing their child into the world. An application for birthing costs can be made, and should be dealt with quickly, although a judge can decide to hold over a ruling on birthing costs until your full case is heard, which could potentially see your child blowing out a candle on a birthday cake before it is resolved.

Barring and safety orders

These types of order can be applied for at any court. However, if your case is already being heard in a particular court, you may have to apply to that court.

A safety order is an order of the court that tells a person who is violent that he or she must desist from any further violence, or indeed any threats of violence or intimidating behaviour. This order does not mean that your spouse will have to leave the family home if you are still living together, but it will formally instruct him or her to behave in an acceptable manner. If a safety order is put in place against your spouse when s/he is no longer living in your home, s/he will not be allowed in the immediate vicinity of your home, unless to take up another order of the court such as access. If taking up an access order under the terms of a safety order, s/he must behave in a cordial and unthreatening manner at collection and drop-off times.

A barring order, on the other hand, is an order which compels the violent person to leave the family home and will also bar them from being in the direct vicinity of that home.

In order to get either a safety order or a barring order, you will have to make an application to the court. If there is a waiting time for your case to be heard, the court may see fit to grant a protection order. A protection order has the same remit as a safety order and goes into effect immediately, giving you time to seek a formal safety order. There is the same recourse with a barring order: the court can grant an interim barring order, which takes effect immediately, pending a hearing for a full barring order.

The advantage of having such orders in place is that, if you do run into difficulty and have to call for assistance, it is much easier for the gardaí to act upon your call, regardless of whether they witnessed any violent act, if one occurred, as it would be clear that the person concerned is in breach of the order by being at or in your home.

[8]

OTHER LESSONS
I LEARNED
ABOUT THE
COURTS

We have looked at what it is like to be in a courtroom and what issues a court most commonly makes orders in connection with, and you would think that that would be everything. If only it could be that simple. The court processes are often cumbersome and imperfect. To give you an example, after I was granted my divorce it took nearly four months, with numerous visits by my solicitor to the courts, before I could get the court order showing I was divorced. So you see, despite procedures being in place, not everything runs smoothly all the time.

I am going to describe some of the pitfalls you may encounter, so that you can ensure that they do not happen to you – if you are representing yourself – or your legal team. Remember, the more mistakes that are made along the way, the more it is going to cost you financially. If you have to go back to court to deal with something that should have been addressed at an earlier court appearance, you will have to pay for that additional time – not many people work for free.

What is a court order?

The court clerk makes a note of the judgments of the court during a court case. These judgments are then listed in a court order, a copy of which will be made available to both sides. The court order will state the names of the applicant and respondent, the date of the case, the name of the judge, the record number of your case and the name of the barristers or legal representatives. This is followed by a definitive list of items that the court ordered. When you receive a copy of the order, it will be signed and attested by the county registrar, thus proving it is an actual order of the court.

What if the court order is incorrect when you receive a copy of it?

This is something that most people would think could never happen. However, occasionally it does. If you are unfortunate enough for it to happen to you, there are a couple of things you can do. Your solicitor can write to the opposing side making them aware of the error, and, if both sides agree, an application can be made back to the court to have the court order amended to reflect the omission. Your presence will not be required in court to do this, just the applicant's and/or the respondent's solicitor. If, however, as can happen, the opposing side disagrees with your contention, you will have to make an application to appear back before the judge to remind him/her of the order they made and ask for an amended order. Most judges take notes throughout each case, so it should simply be a case of the judge referring to his/her notes to ensure s/he did actually make the order. However, it may take some time to get back in front of the judge – it would certainly be unlikely to happen within a matter of days – and you may have to wait until the following term before being able to make the application.

What if the court will not decide upon the issues before it?

If the court will not decide upon the issues before it, do not panic. Decisions relating to certain matters can be held off until the final decision is made about the terms of your separation. This enables an overall decision to be made in relation to all the issues as a whole. Unfortunately, this can sometimes see you waiting many months, if not years, for some decisions to be reached.

What to do if you are unhappy with any of the orders

If you are unhappy with an order the court has made, you have a right to appeal. Once the order is issued (which is the day in court when the judge makes the order, not when you get the paper copy of the order), you have a period of ten working days to lodge an appeal against the order. If an appeal is lodged, a new court date will be sought and your appeal, and the basis for it, will be heard. It will not be heard by the same judge, but by a higher court – if you wish to appeal an award made in the circuit court, you would have to appeal it to the high court. The down side is that an appearance in the high court is more expensive than one in the circuit court, and for this reason many people who are unhappy with a court order do not appeal it – they simply cannot afford to.

I have known people who could not afford to appeal an order to wait for a period of time and then reapply to the same court for a variation in the existing order, for the same reasons that they would have used to appeal the order. Some of these were successful, others were not.

What a court does if you breach any of the above orders

If you breach a court order, the court can hold you in contempt for breach of an order and place you in custody. As I mentioned above, a family law court may be more lenient than a criminal one. If a court order is repeatedly broken by one party, the other party can seek to have a committal order served against that party. This is an order seeking to have that party imprisoned for breach of a court order. The fact that you seek such an order does not necessarily mean that the offending party will automatically be sent to prison, but it gives the court the option to decide whether or not to do so.

Does the cost of going to court outweigh the benefits?

I am asked this question a lot, and I have to say that I don't have a simple yes or no answer. I tell everyone to do everything humanly possible not to go to court – try to sort out the issues between yourselves or with the help of a mediator. If this fails, there are two options: do nothing or go to court. If you find yourself between a rock and a hard place, you don't have a choice if you want to resolve the situation. However, if you find yourself in court because you were too proud to sit down with your estranged spouse and negotiate an agreement, you may regret it when you see your legal bills starting to mount up. Without legal aid, both sides jointly could easily spend anywhere between €10,000 and €50,000. Couldn't you think of better ways of spending that money?

My top ten trivia

1. The district court does not hear full judicial separation hearings – you have to apply to the circuit court.

2. District courts will deal with maintenance, barring orders and a host of other items.

3. Courts can make errors in relation to paperwork. Make sure you keep copies of everything.

4. All the court clerks I dealt with were wonderful, helpful people, offering a greatly under-rated service. They were sympathetic stewards along the road and helped ease the journey.

5. If you don't ask for something, it won't be awarded. Make sure you ask for all the reliefs you need, so that the court can deal with them.

6. Try not to overwhelm people with too much information. While you may know your case inside out, do not assume that everyone else will remember the details with as much accuracy.

7. If your legal team gets it wrong, tell them.

8. Even if you are given a court date in the courtroom, always check with the court clerks several weeks prior to your case that it is actually listed for the date you think it is.

9. Be prepared to wait around for your case to be heard, and for a possible adjournment.

10. Bring something to read or distract you, in case you have to wait around. You could even bring a CD player (with headphones!) so you can listen to some music.

[9]

WORKING OUT YOUR FINANCES

This chapter is intended to help you work out what your new financial needs and responsibilities are going to be once you move forward as a single person. While many may be interested in getting as much as they feasibly can out of the financial pot, I would urge you to try to be realistic. No judge will be impressed by someone fabricating claims as to what they need. Let us consider a hypothetical situation. If one party listed an expenditure of €40 a month for herself and her two children on toiletries, which would include shampoo, toothpaste, stuff for the kids and general medicines for herself and her children, and the other party listed an expenditure of €60 a month for aftershave and general vanity products, which do you think would look more reasonable in the eyes of a judge? The cheaper claim catering for three people or the greater claim catering for one?

As tedious as it may be to sit down and go through your monthly expenditure with a fine-tooth comb, it is probably one of the first things you will be asked to do. Your solicitor will require these figures in order to assess your case. The formal legal document which will be presented in court outlining your financial position is known as an 'affidavit of means'. Your solicitor will provide you with a blank affidavit of means form for completion by you, possibly with some guidelines.

Affidavit of means

An affidavit of means is a sworn document. Essentially, this means that you swear that all the information in it is true and you sign your name to it in the presence of a commissioner for oaths or practising solicitor, who witnesses that you have signed your name (proof of identity may be required) and that you are aware of all the contents of the document. A sworn document can then become a document which can be used by the courts, as it is as reliable and legally binding as if you had stood in the court and verbally sworn an oath that all the contents of the document are true. A court will require that all documents before it are sworn, so that they can be treated as true statements when a decision is being made regarding the facts contained within the document.

The affidavit of means will be one of the documents presented in court and made available to the other side in order to determine the division of assets and possible award of maintenance. Both sides will see each other's affidavit of means and, indeed, all documents that are intended for use in court, so both sides will have knowledge of what the other party is claiming prior to going to court.

An affidavit of means will give full details of all your personal assets, your sources of income, debts and/or liabilities, your monthly, weekly and yearly personal outgoings and expenses and your pension scheme, if you have one. All documents used in the court follow a set format; you just have to fill in the blanks. Below is an example of an affidavit of means form. Have a look at it and see what you would list in each section. Then turn to page 125 and see one that I have completed. Compare it with what you would have listed and see if you have considered all your possible outgoings. Mine may not have covered everything – indeed you may come up with more – but it should give you some guidance as to which items you should consider for inclusion.

When complete, this document is signed in the presence of a commissioner for oaths. The cost of swearing a document is just a few euro.

An example of an affidavit of means form

AN CHÚIRT TEAGHLAIGH CHUARDA
(THE CIRCUIT FAMILY COURT)

(*Name of circuit court*) CIRCUIT
COUNTY OF (*name of county*)

IN THE MATTER OF THE FAMILY LAW
(DIVORCE) ACT, 1996

BETWEEN
(Insert the name of the applicant – person applying to court.)

Applicant

AND

(Insert the name of the person who is responding.)

Respondent

AFFIDAVIT OF MEANS

I, (insert the applicant's name, address and occupation), aged 18 years and upwards MAKE OATH and say as follows:

1. I say that I am the Applicant/Respondent (*delete as appropriate*) in the above entitled proceedings and I make the Affidavit from facts within my own knowledge save where otherwise appears and where so appearing, I believe the same to be true.
2. I say that I have set out in the First Schedule hereto all the assets to which I am legally or beneficially entitled and the manner in which such property is held.
3. I say that I have set out in the Second Schedule hereto all income which I receive and the source(s) of such income.
4. I say that I have set out in the Third Schedule hereto all my debts and/or liabilities and the persons to whom such debts and liabilities are due.
5. I say that my weekly/monthly (*delete as appropriate*) outgoings amount to the sum of (*insert actual figure*) and I say that the details of such outgoings have been set out in the Fourth Schedule hereto.
6. I say that to the best of my knowledge, information and belief, all pension information known to me relevant to the within proceedings is set out in the Fifth Schedule hereto. [Details should be attached from the trustees of the pension scheme outlining your benefits and, where such information is not attached, the reasons should be given as to why such information has not been obtained.]

FIRST SCHEDULE
ASSETS OF THE APPLICANT

[This is where you list all assets held both solely in your own name and in joint names with your spouse and/or any other individual.]

SECOND SCHEDULE
INCOME OF THE APPLICANT/RESPONDENT

[This is where you list all sources and amounts of income, whether they are social welfare payments, salary, incoming rent or income from any other source such as shares, rent, etc.]

THIRD SCHEDULE
DEBTS AND/OR LIABILITIES OF
APPLICANT/RESPONDENT

[This is where you list all debts and liabilities. Even if you are not servicing some of the debts, such as a mortgage or a holiday loan for example, once the debt is legally in your name, jointly or solely, you should list it. These debts may include such things as mortgage repayments, loans, credit card debts, bank loans, Credit Union loans, personal loans from family, loans taken out through employment sources, etc.]

FOURTH SCHEDULE
WEEKLY/MONTHLY PERSONAL OUTGOINGS
OF THE APPLICANT/RESPONDENT

[List all weekly and monthly outgoings that you have. It may also be useful to list all the annual expenses that you have, for example car insurance, motor tax, etc. You can then divide annual expenses by either fifty-two or twelve, depending on whether you are listing your outgoings on a monthly or weekly basis.]

FIFTH SCHEDULE
PENSION SCHEME DETAILS

[Insert all pension details as per the trustees of your pension scheme.]

DECLARED before me by the said
(*insert your name here*)

who is personally known to me
(or who is identified to me by)

(*Insert the name of the person who identifies you, their address and occupation.*)

This (date) day of (month), 20_____

_____

Commissioner for Oaths/Practising Solicitor

Signed: _____

(*your name*)
Applicant

It may seem like a lot of information, but it is not such a daunting task as you may think. I strongly suggest you find a quiet time to complete this, then put it to one side and review it at a later date prior to sending it to your solicitor. No one can really tell you what you should remember to include in these schedules, as no one knows your financial situation or needs as well as you do. Do listen to suggestions from your solicitor as to what s/he thinks you should include or exclude.

Points to bear in mind when working out your finances

~ Some bills vary from month to month; for example, heating costs are higher in the winter than in the summer. In such instances, it is a good idea to work out an average monthly amount based on the previous year's bills (divide the total annual amount by twelve).

~ List your costs according to how you receive your income. If you are paid monthly, you should list your expenses on a monthly basis and, if you are paid weekly, you should list them on a weekly basis. It helps to build a clearer picture if you match your income against your expenditure.

~ While making sure you include all your actual costs, try to be realistic about what you include. Don't embellish the list in any shape or form. Only one item needs to be shown to be totally incorrect to discredit you in the eyes of the court. So, if you haven't worked out in a gym for the last ten years, suddenly including an annual membership subscription for one is a bit unrealistic.

~ Avoid getting involved in a bidding war, trying to out-manoeuvre your spouse with an even greater list of expenses. Concentrate on your own financial position.

~ Be realistic, and as accurate as it is possible to be. If you need to build in a bit of contingency, do so under a truthful heading (e.g. it is reasonable to include an annual cost for car maintenance, or for the servicing of your gas boiler, or for future potential costs such as your car's NCT, etc.).

∼ Some costs may currently be shared, or one spouse may be bearing them in full. List these expenses, so that both you and your solicitor are aware of all potential costs in the future. Your solicitor will advise you as to what is appropriate in the final affidavit. If your partner is paying the car loan, for example, but you are going to take over the use of the car solely, you may be liable for these costs in the settlement.

∼ Even if you are not servicing a debt or loan, once it is in your name it can be legally recovered against you, so you should include any debts that fit into this category.

∼ When you calculate all the totals, make sure you recheck them and add them up again. It is amazing how many people miscalculate the totals and present inaccurate affidavits – a point which will quickly be picked up by the opposing side, as they will also cross-reference your figures and total to make sure they are correct and accurate. Take the time to make sure your financial calculations are correct – don't presume your solicitor will check them for you.

∼ It is a good idea to give your solicitor as clear a picture as possible of your finances. You should discuss and review the completed affidavit with your solicitor prior to swearing it with a commissioner for oaths. Once this affidavit is sworn and presented in court, it becomes a legal document which you are accountable for and could have to answer questions on – so take the time to make sure it is correct.

~ Where possible, try to provide – or at least have to hand – any original documents to substantiate your claim (e.g. phone bill, credit card statements, medical receipts, etc.). Then, if a question arises as to their validity, your barrister will be able to provide direct proof.

~ When a judicial separation is applied for, the courts will usually order each side to disclose certain financial paperwork to the other side. They may order that you disclose financial statements covering a number of years, anything from bank statements to credit card statements – whatever is appropriate. This helps both sides to build up a picture of their spending patterns and make sure that subsequent claims are realistic. You can also apply to the court for an order of discovery against the opposing side for disclosure of relevant financial statements.

~ You should take the time to sit down and read a copy of your spouse's affidavit of means. This will be sent to your solicitor prior to the court case and your solicitor should make it available to you for your review and comments. You know your spouse, and you will probably know if his/her affidavit is realistic – if their claim is somewhat inflated or, more importantly, if anything has been omitted from the list of assets or liabilities. The picture each of you paints in your affidavit of means will have a bearing on the other.

Some honest advice

~ Don't waste your time preparing an affidavit of means that does not reflect the truth. Remember, a lie told and proven in court can completely discredit you. Both of you will probably have a good idea of what the other's financial position really is, so do credit each other with a bit of intelligence.

~ Don't hide or omit to declare financial accounts. If you refuse to provide the paperwork, the other side may seek a subpoena against a financial institution to provide the financial statements and they would have to comply.

~ Don't, on threat of court proceedings, run up an overdraft on your account or run up huge debts, as the court will compare such debts with the timing of your separation. The court will know from this whether you are being in any way 'creative' with your accounting for the purposes of misleading the court.

~ If you are a PAYE worker and do not declare your full income, the other side may subpoena your employer, who will then be obliged to testify in court as to what your earnings really are.

~ Once the affidavit is sworn and submitted, or lodged in court, you cannot change it. You will be held accountable for all it contains. By 'lodged in court' I mean that all original legal documentation to be used in the court will first be lodged with the court office and copies bearing the court stamp will be served on the other side. In this way, both parties will have copies of the opposing side's documents and the originals lodged in the court office will be available for the judge to read prior to or during your case.

~ If there is a change in your finances between submitting your affidavit and appearing in court, your barrister can bring it to the court's attention.

~ Be honest. It's better for everyone – emotionally and financially – in the long run.

There follows an example of a completed affidavit of means. It is by no means fully inclusive of all possible items but is intended to act as a memory jogger, to help kick-start the process for you.

An example of a completed affidavit of means form

AN CHÚIRT TEAGHLAIGH CHUARDA (THE CIRCUIT FAMILY COURT)

(*Name of circuit court*) CIRCUIT
COUNTY OF (*name of county*)

IN THE MATTER OF THE FAMILY LAW (DIVORCE) ACT, 1996

BETWEEN

Josephine Bloggs
Applicant
AND
John Bloggs
Respondent

AFFIDAVIT OF MEANS

I, **Josephine Bloggs**, aged 18 years and upwards MAKE OATH and say as follows:

1. I say that I am the Applicant in the above entitled proceedings and I make the Affidavit from facts within my own knowledge save where otherwise appears and where so appearing, I believe the same to be true.

2. I say that I have set out in the First Schedule hereto all the assets to which I am legally or beneficially entitled and the manner in which such property is held.

3. I say that I have set out in the Second Schedule hereto all income which I receive and the source(s) of such income.

4. I say that I have set out in the Third Schedule hereto all my debts and/or liabilities and the persons to whom such debts and liabilities are due.

5. I say that my monthly outgoings amount to the sum of (*insert figure*) euro and I say that the details of such outgoings have been set out in the Fourth Schedule hereto.

6. I say that to the best of my knowledge, information and belief, all pension information known to me relevant to the within proceedings is set out in the Fifth Schedule hereto. [Details should be attached from the trustees of the pension scheme outlining your benefits and, where such information is not attached, the reasons should be given as to why such information has not been obtained.]

FIRST SCHEDULE
ASSETS OF THE APPLICANT   €

1. Property at 1 Main Street, Dublin
2. Contents of property at 1 Main Street, Dublin
3. Ford Fiesta 1 litre 2000 car
4. Shares in XYZ Ltd – current market value
5. SSIA savings account with XYZ Bank
6. Current account with XYZ Bank
7. Deposit account with XYZ Bank
8. Share options in company
9. Three paintings valued at
10. Jewellery

 Total

(*This is not a complete list, and you may have only one or even no assets, but be aware of all the things that are considered to be assets. Anything that has substantial value that can be realised is an asset.*)

SECOND SCHEDULE
INCOME OF THE
APPLICANT/RESPONDENT   €

Social welfare payments

Monthly wage

Children's allowance

Income from a rental property

Dividends received from shares, etc.

Overtime

Bonus payments received from employer

Income for room rented at above property

Expense account from employer

Car allowance from employer

(Anything that puts money in your hand on a weekly, monthly or yearly basis is considered income. Even state-assisted payments are considered to be income.)

THIRD SCHEDULE
DEBTS AND/OR LIABILITIES OF
APPLICANT/RESPONDENT   €

Mortgage (the actual amount of the mortgage
loan for your home that is still outstanding)
Credit card debt
Car loan
Credit Union loan (holiday loan, etc.)
Any other bank loans
Student loan still outstanding
Any debt outstanding with any of the utility companies
– such as phone, ESB, etc. – should also be included

(Any legal debt – i.e. which can be legally recovered from you – should be listed as a debt. Anything that you have a liability to pay is a debt. Do not include weekly or monthly future debts – such as food, etc. – here, as they are listed in the next schedule. This schedule also refers to the overall amount of the outstanding debt – not the weekly/monthly amount payable to service the debt.)

FOURTH SCHEDULE
WEEKLY/MONTHLY PERSONAL OUTGOINGS
OF THE APPLICANT/RESPONDENT   €

Rent
Monthly mortgage payment
Monthly credit card payment
Food
ESB
Gas
Phone (land line and mobile)

Cable

House insurance

Health insurance

Life insurance

Car insurance (annual figure divided by either twelve or fifty-two)

Car maintenance

Car tax

Crèche fees and babysitting

School fees (annual figure divided by either twelve or fifty-two)

Petrol/monthly bus pass or train ticket

Medical expenses (doctors' visits for yourself or the children)

Any ongoing prescription costs

Other house costs (maintenance, refuse charges, etc.)

Annual memberships

Professional membership

College courses, if studying

All loan repayments

Newspapers

Toiletries (including prescriptions, etc.)

Any pension contributions

Clothes for self

Clothes for children

Shoes for self and children

School uniforms

School books

Extra-curricular activities for children

TV licence

All annual costs (broken down into cost per week or month)

FIFTH SCHEDULE
PENSION SCHEME DETAILS   **€**

[Insert all pension details as per the trustees of your pension scheme.]

DECLARED before me by the said
(*insert your name here*)

who is personally known to me
(or who is identified to me by)

(*Insert the name of the person who identifies you, their address and occupation.*)

This (date) day of (month), 20_____

_____

Commissioner for Oaths/Practising Solicitor

Signed: _____

(*your name*)
Applicant

Now that you have completed the practical side of sitting down and working out all your expenses, you will have a clear idea of either the amount of maintenance you will require or the amount of maintenance you may be liable to pay. The total outstanding amount – i.e. the difference between your income and expenditure – is not necessarily what you will be awarded or be ordered to pay. What one spouse can afford to pay will be balanced against the other's needs.

I have heard it said that one of the top three causes of arguments in a marriage is money. It is probably true to say that, if it was a contentious issue when you were married, it is likely to be even more contentious now that you are separated. While a court will try to ensure that both parties are provided for, and of paramount importance will be the welfare of the children of the marriage, there are some things that you should be realistic about. Two people living together is cheaper than two people living apart. Once you divide the two lives, you also divide assets and inevitably increase costs. This usually means that the lifestyles of both parties will be compromised somewhere along the line, as the available disposable income suddenly has greater pressures put on it.

Manage your expectations and plan for the future

The division of assets, such as a family home or a business, once done, is unlikely to be reviewed or changed in the future. It is possible to apply for a re-division of the proceeds, but this is likely to be an uphill struggle.

An order for ongoing maintenance is made according to the needs of both spouses at the time and the financial ability of one of the spouses to support the other. However, each party always has 'liberty to apply', which means the freedom to apply for a maintenance order to be altered if there is a change in either party's circumstances. For instance, if the spouse paying maintenance is made redundant, an application can be made to reduce the liability for maintenance. The spouse in receipt of maintenance can ask for the original order to be reinstated once the unemployed spouse finds new employment. If the party paying maintenance were to have a sudden increase in earnings – e.g. by obtaining a better-paid job – the other spouse could apply for a greater amount of that salary. Also, if the party in receipt of maintenance is not working but subsequently obtains employment, the other party may seek a reduction in the maintenance s/he is paying.

If one party was receiving a tax allowance as a married couple and his/her tax status changes as a result of the separation, that party may now be taxed as a single person, thus reducing the amount of net take-home pay.

The needs of both parties have to be matched to the amount of finances available. If you are seeking a maintenance order for a sum that your spouse does not have the financial means to pay, then a court is hardly going to make an order for that amount. However, in such an instance, the spouse in receipt of maintenance is free to seek an alternative remedy, such as an increased percentage of the assets by way of a lump sum advance payment.

Unless you are both in the enviable position of having huge financial resources, your lifestyle is going to have to change to accommodate your new circumstances.

Entitlement to maintenance or liability to pay may also be influenced by potential future earnings. If, for argument's sake, one party is in the final stages of any form of education, whether it be a degree or a new trade, the future earning potential of that spouse may well be relevant when a court is making a decision about maintenance. If one party has gone out to work in order to support the other party in furthering their education, s/he may be entitled to receive some of the future earning potential of the newly qualified spouse, given that they would not have been in that position without them.

Personal circumstances vary from case to case and the court may take different things into consideration, such as:

∼ One party stayed at home and may have sacrificed a career in order to raise the children of the marriage or look after a disabled parent.

~ The parties have a shared business to which they have both contributed.

~ One party may have used an amount of money bequeathed directly to them to clear the mortgage and thus reduced the financial liabilities of the 'couple'.

Always make sure your solicitor is aware of any personal circumstances which you feel may be relevant.

Whilst finances are finances and hard figures are difficult to argue with, the circumstances surrounding them will differ from couple to couple. So while you may list an affidavit of income and expenditure, make sure your solicitor has a fuller understanding as to why your financial circumstances are as they are. You never really know what the court may find pertinent.

Other financial aspects to consider

While you take the time to consider the new financial position you find yourself in as a result of separating, you should bear in mind how this will affect your income, not from the point of view of income and expenditure but in terms of your new tax situation and any allowances you now qualify for or risk losing as a result. For example, if as a spouse you are in receipt of maintenance for yourself but not your children, this may be subject to tax. If you are applying for social welfare payments, the Department of Social, Community and Family Affairs may require that you apply for maintenance for your children before they will consider your entitlement to claim for certain social welfare payments. You may be required to provide proof that you have indeed sought maintenance payments. A person in receipt of social welfare payments who is liable for making maintenance payments may be entitled to an allowance for a dependent spouse and/or children. This portion of the allowance, where a court order for maintenance exists, can be paid directly to the dependent spouse. A married spouse who is available for and seeking work may also be considered for unemployment benefit.

While everyone's financial position differs, it is wise to contact the Department of Social Welfare and/or your tax office to discover if there are any allowances that you are entitled to claim. A phone call that will take up very little of your time can be time well spent and may have an influence on what you need to achieve from a court settlement. If you are paying maintenance or are in receipt of it, you should check what your tax position is in relation to this – whether the maintenance payments are taxable income. This situation may change from one government budget to another.

Seek the advice of an accountant

If you do not take into account any possible tax liability you may have, your potential disposable income may be reduced, so you should consult an accountant for advice in relation to this. You could also contact the Money Advice Budgeting Service (MABS). The primary aim of MABS is to help people cope with debt and take control of their own finances. The service is free, confidential and independent. You can find out more about MABS on their website (www.mabs.ie) or by contacting them directly. There are sixty-five centres throughout Ireland.

[10]

THE
MAINTENANCE
MYTH

In most fairy stories the prince rides in on a white charger, colours blazing, to rescue the downtrodden princess from a fate worse than death. He whisks her off to his castle, where she lives happily ever after without a care in the world. The prince always seems to be tall, dark and handsome and invariably protects his family from all the evils of the world. He usually has a great pad and drives the latest model in white chargers. If only life could be like that, we sigh. But now is the time for a reality check! When the dust has settled on a separation, there are some things that don't just come to an end as soon as a court order is made. The main issues that live on are access and maintenance. Both these may see you making repeated court appearances for many years to come.

Like many of the issues involved in separation, these have the potential to be highly contentious. In a changing world, where often both parties work and have careers, maintenance is something which may be sought by either party. There are many myths circulating about maintenance: tales of people in receipt of vast sums of maintenance while ex-spouses are destitute; tales of parents who never see a penny and raise their children without any financial help from their ex-spouse. These are cautionary tales indeed.

While not entering into debate about the rights or wrongs of custody awards, it is a fact that the majority of custody awards are made to mothers, with fathers having access rights. This means that the onus of seeking maintenance for children usually falls on mothers, as it is the custodial parent that has to ensure that the children are adequately catered for.

I have found that there are three types of maintenance payer. There are those parents who, despite no longer living on a full-time basis with their children, do their utmost to ensure that their family is properly provided for. I have met many who fall into this category and many custodial parents who acknowledge this fact gratefully.

The second type needs to be taken to court in order to reach a financial settlement in relation to maintenance. However, once ordered to do so, they do honour the commitment, even if some make frequent applications to vary the maintenance award (which doesn't usually mean applying to increase their contribution). Despite this reluctance, at the end of the day they do actually support their kids financially.

The third kind – and, sadly, it has to be acknowledged that they do exist – is the ex-partner who refuses to pay maintenance, even when the maintenance is only for the children. This is the kind of parent who, even when ordered by the court to pay maintenance, deliberately defies the court and refuses to comply with the order. Some single custodial parents even have to have more than one job just to make ends meet, having simply given up chasing the ever-elusive maintenance payment.

You may read the last paragraph and think that this could never happen to you or your children. But remember, nothing changes a relationship like a separation. And there was a time when you thought you would never have to face separation. Much of this book is about managing your expectations in the whole process, which is why I suggest you identify which type of maintenance payer you are dealing with. Burying your head in the sand won't make this issue go away, and it's best to know what you are dealing with up front so that you can make decisions accordingly.

The technical part

There are lots of questions that are frequently asked in relation to maintenance – I know I had a list as long as my arm – so let us look at some of the concerns I had and some of the answers I became aware of during the process.

Who pays maintenance?

Both parents are responsible for the maintenance of any children of the marriage. The actual level of maintenance each parent may be liable to pay is directly proportional to their ability to pay. If one parent is not working, the liability of the second – working – parent may increase, as his/her maintenance payments may have to cater for both the children and the ex-spouse.

Who can apply for maintenance in relation to the children of a marriage?

The custodial parent (the parent with whom the children reside) or the legal guardian of the children may apply for maintenance.

Can I claim maintenance even if we have no children?

There are a number of factors to be considered when there are no children of the marriage. If one spouse is not in a position to work – due to age, poor health or any other relevant reason – then the other spouse may be liable to pay maintenance to support him/her. This may change – for instance, if the spouse regains full health and returns to work, or undergoes further education in order to get employment.

What if we are still sharing the family home?

Even if the two spouses still share the family home, maintenance may still have to be paid. Couples often separate and, until the situation is resolved from a legal perspective, remain living under one roof. This can still count as a separation in the eyes of the law and a liability for maintenance may ensue, as spousal and child maintenance can still be applied for in these circumstances.

How much maintenance can be claimed?

The court you apply to in relation to the issue of maintenance directly affects the award that can be made. If you make an application that is heard in the district court, at the time of writing, the maximum award of maintenance the judge can make for each child is €150 a week, and €500 per week for the spouse. If your application is heard in the circuit court, there is no upper limit imposed on the amount the judge can award for the maintenance of your children. These are the initial parameters.

For how long can I claim maintenance?

In relation to any children of the marriage, maintenance can be claimed until the children reach eighteen years of age, or twenty-three if in full-time education.

Factors a court may consider in relation to child maintenance payments

When an order for maintenance for the support of children is being awarded, the court will take into account the following key factors.

~ The needs of the children.

~ The potential ability of the liable spouse to meet the payments.

~ The current lifestyles of the children, which the court will endeavour not to change unless the court feels there is no other option.

~ The age of the children and whether the custodial parent is working or not. In other words, if a custodial spouse was working full-time while the family was still together, the court is highly unlikely to make an award which suddenly allows him/her to stay at home with the children and no longer work.

In many situations, the custodial parent finds him or herself in a position where s/he is forced to go back to work in order to make ends meet.

Factors you should bear in mind that are outside the court's remit

Let us go back to one of the first considerations of the court: the person's ability to pay. If the spouse is unemployed, has no other financial assets and is claiming social welfare (either unemployment benefit or unemployment assistance), an application can be made for an increased payment due to the fact that he/she has dependent children. The maximum additional amount which can be claimed for dependent children through social welfare payments is €16.80.

If your ex-spouse claims financial poverty, the onus is on you to prove otherwise and, if you cannot, the likelihood is that a smaller maintenance award will be made. This is despite the fact that the basic needs of you and your children will not change in line with the amount of money that can be provided. What is more, if the financial situation of your ex-spouse improves, you can only seek to change the maintenance award by going back to court and subsequently incurring more legal costs.

Remedies if an ex-spouse does not pay

If the maintenance-paying ex-spouse decides not to pay the maintenance order, there are a number of things that can happen.

~ You can seek another court date in order to bring it to the court's attention that the maintenance order is in default and therefore seek to have it enforced. Given that it is a family law situation, the courts are usually lenient regarding the first couple of breaches of maintenance payments. The judge may simply instruct the ex-spouse to make amends, pay the arrears and continue paying the maintenance – cold comfort if you are struggling to meet bills.

~ If you go back to court to seek both the arrears and continued payments, the other party can seek a variance of the maintenance order and you may walk away with a decreased order. This is only likely to happen if there has been a significant change in that spouse's financial circumstances.

~ If the maintenance-paying spouse has a record of defaulting and is in gainful employment (this is not applicable to self-employed people), you can seek a 'garnishee order' (attachment of earnings summons), which is an order made by the court instructing the company your spouse works for to deduct the maintenance amount at source and pay it directly to you. This guarantees that your maintenance will be received on a regular basis. The only negative side to this is that, if your ex-spouse chooses to change employment, the garnishee order does not automatically transfer to the new company. You would have to seek a new/amended court order against the new place of employment, which could put you under considerable financial strain, as every court appearance for an amendment of an order can cost money if you are not in receipt of legal aid. However, this should be brought to the court's attention at the hearing of your case.

~ In a district court, if there have been problems with payment of maintenance, the court may make an order that the maintenance is to be lodged with the court clerk, who will then make it available to the person receiving maintenance.

~ Sometimes a spouse in receipt of maintenance may decide that the cost of pursuing maintenance outweighs the benefits of receiving it. I have met many custodial parents who have come to the conclusion that they are simply wasting their time and money chasing the elusive.

~ It may be more difficult to enforce a maintenance order against someone who is self-employed and defaults.

Arrears of maintenance

In the district court, if the maintenance-paying spouse falls into arrears and the spouse in receipt of maintenance wishes to make a claim, the Enforcement of Court Orders Act (1940) limits the recovery of arrears to those which have accrued in the six months immediately prior to issuing proceedings.

The circuit court can make an order that any amount is owing on foot of its existing order. This would be subject to the court being satisfied as to the actual sum owing. However, it may be more difficult to establish default over a very long period.

Costs in relation to seeking arrears on maintenance

Any party making an application to court will usually include an application for the costs associated with that court appearance. If the reason for making the application is repeated default by the other party, then the court may make the defaulting party liable for all costs (on both sides) in relation to the application. While this does happen, and such awards are made, if a defaulting party claims s/he is unable to pay, it will hardly be feasible to make him/her liable for another debt. If you have a solicitor and costs are awarded against the other side, you are still primarily liable for your solicitor's costs.

Can an appeal be made to the court by the maintenance-paying spouse?

Either party has the right to make an appeal to the court in relation to a maintenance order. As maintenance is ongoing over the course of many years, it is often subject to change. Maintenance payments may be increased in line with changing personal circumstances, rises in the cost of living, inflation, illness and many other factors. Just as they can be appealed to be increased, they can also be appealed to be decreased for much the same reasons, and indeed many more.

If my spouse no longer lives in Ireland, can I still pursue maintenance payments?

You can pursue maintenance payments from a spouse living in the UK or any EU country. A maintenance order issued by any court in Ireland can be served through any magistrate's court in the UK. You would, however, need an address or place of employment, or some other way of contacting the spouse who is no longer resident in Ireland. While the law clearly makes provisions for and will assist in the recovery of maintenance from the spouse who leaves the country, it may in reality prove very difficult. I am not just talking about it being difficult from a financial perspective (although that is also a factor), but from a practical perspective, as it may take a great deal of time and effort to track down the spouse. And what is the other person supposed to do in the meantime? Cases where both parties reside in Ireland can take long enough, let alone when one of the parties no longer resides here.

Interim maintenance orders

An application can be made to the courts for an 'interim maintenance order'. The hearing for such an application will usually be scheduled more quickly than a full separation hearing, as the need is more immediate. An interim order will be put in place to address the applicant's immediate needs until a final award is made at the full hearing of the case. It can be dealt with on its own and does not have to be heard in conjunction with the rest of the case.

Other options besides maintenance

As stated earlier, each parent has an automatic legal liability in relation to the maintenance of their children. However, whilst a court will not negate this liability, either party may put forward other suggestions on how to meet this liability. Obviously this depends on the financial assets of the marriage and of each individual, but, if you can offer an alternative solution to either receiving maintenance or meeting your obligation to pay it, you should discuss this with your solicitor and explore it as a possibility. The worst the court can do is say no.

Thinking outside the box – some alternative options you could explore

Always remain open to exploring new ways of doing things. It is a good idea to sit down and try to come up with options that you would not have considered before. Looking at things in a different way may help you come up with a better solution, which you could then discuss with your legal team.

> ∼ If, for example, there is one family home, with a set amount of equity, there is a possibility that the home may be sold and the proceeds divided. However, the spouse found liable to pay maintenance could sign away his/her rights to that home and the other person could take that share of the equity as payment of maintenance for an agreed period of time – say five, eight or ten years, depending on the amount of equity. This would, however, be an unusual scenario, but the point of suggesting

it is to illustrate how it can be possible to find a more creative solution.

~ While each case has a different list of assets, each couple may be willing to accept different things. When you initially talk to a solicitor, s/he will routinely address the issues of maintenance, the family home, etc., in order to assess how the assets are to be divided and who will be liable to pay maintenance. However, each couple's needs are different – everyone has different priorities – so, if there is an alternative solution that would suit you, make sure you discuss it with your solicitor.

~ Not every spouse will want to receive maintenance, and this is obviously easier where no children are involved. Added to which, both parties may want to sever all contact with the other. However, you cannot sign away your right to claim maintenance where children are involved, in which case a lump sum payment, such as equity, would mean that, in essence, any maintenance liability has been met in advance.

Costs in relation to seeking maintenance

If you cannot afford to pay a solicitor to seek maintenance or arrears of maintenance, you can seek an order for maintenance on your own, without legal representation (see Chapter 4).

Maintenance and access

I have often listened to debates on both maintenance and access – fathers talking about their rights to see their children and women discussing their right to receive financial help from the father of their children. Yet, access and maintenance are not in any way linked. One is not dependent on the other, nor should a failure in one be an excuse for refusing the other. This is for very sound reasons: the benefit of the children. This is not to detract in any way from the hardship one spouse may suffer as a result of the actions of the other. As hard as it can be, it is better not to link these two in your mind.

[11]

ACCESS

A ccess is often a hotly debated topic in the newspapers today, particularly in relation to fathers and what they feel their rights to be. It can be a highly emotional issue, particularly when there is a lot of acrimony between the two parents. A parent who feels his/her role is under threat will fight hard. When you think about it, time spent with one parent can sometimes mean less time spent with the other. Not being able to see a child because it is not your 'time' can be emotionally very hard for both parents.

The debate around access issues could fill this entire book, and that would defeat its purpose, so I will simply describe the subject in terms of the court experience and some of the ways I believe it is possible to work through it.

The facts about access

The court has the power to make, and indeed refuse, an award of access to the non-custodial guardian or parent. An access order is a court order outlining the times when that parent can see his/her children. It may also cover such things as holiday arrangements – access during school holidays, Christmas holidays, etc. It will clearly specify when the access times are – for example, every Saturday from 10 a.m. to 7 p.m. If overnight visits are to be allowed, the courts will specify what time the children are to be picked up, when they must be returned and how often the overnight stays are to take place.

Access orders are rarely set in stone, and will change over time according to the age of the children – normally increasing in length as the child gets older – or as the child's changing needs have to be accommodated.

While judges may follow certain guidelines, this does not guarantee consistency in the levels of access given. The decision is dependent on the specific judge and, indeed, the particular details of the case in question. Solicitors and barristers sometimes contend that, depending on what you are looking for, one judge would be more suitable to hear your particular case than another. The court ultimately makes the order based on what it considers to be in the best interests of the children and the parental needs of each parent.

When making a decision in relation to access, the court will normally consider the following factors:

~ The age of the children.

~ Whether or not the parent applying for access has lived with the children and for how long.

~ Depending on the age of the children, the relationship they have with the parent applying for access.

~ The lifestyle of the children and parents involved. This can cover a number of areas, which I will expand on later.

~ The living conditions of the parent applying for access. For example, overnight access may not be allowed if that parent does not have adequate facilities for the child, such as a separate bedroom. If a parent shares a house with other people, this would also be taken into consideration.

~ The reliability, character and background of the parent seeking access. Unless there has been a record of problems or issues that the court would need to take into account in considering access, access is pretty well a certainty.

The best advice I can give anyone who is grappling with the issue of access is to try to take it off the table for discussion. It is hard enough to sort out the financial issues without throwing the issue of access into the pot as well. Do everything possible to sort it out between the two of you, even if you can't agree on any of the other issues. If the two of you find it too hard to sit and discuss it together, consider using a mediator. This could be anyone – a mutual family member or friend that you both trust, your legal team or formal mediation.

Some points to remember when the court is deciding

Make sure both your solicitor and barrister are clear about what you believe are acceptable levels of access and why, in order that they can argue your case in court. A solicitor may advise you as to what is an acceptable level of access in relation to a child of a certain age. However, the lifestyle of both yourself and your child may also be relevant and could change the normal 'acceptable' level of access and how it is awarded.

Do children have a say?

The age at which a court will consider a child's opinion to be valid may vary. Children are generally not asked to give evidence before the court, so a psychologist's report is the usual means of determining a child's point of view (see the section 'Psychologist's reports' on page 154).

We encourage our children to grow up and make their own life choices and we teach them to take responsibility for themselves. This will result in an ever-increasing freedom of choice as they get older. Most children in their late teens have their own friends, their own interests and want to do their own thing at weekends and in their free time after school. If a teenager does not want to visit the other parent at designated access times, it may prove more difficult to try to enforce such an order, as neither the child nor the other parent will find the access as enjoyable. Children of a younger age will not have as active a role to play in determining when and where they see each parent.

How do children have their say?

A very young child – anything from a baby to somewhere between the age of six and eight – will generally have no say as to access arrangements. If the child willingly goes with the non-custodial parent and is happy to spend time with them, there really is no problem. If, however, the child refuses to go, the other parent can enforce the access arrangements and remove the child from the home to avail of the access rights. Courts are far more likely to take into account the views of children of, say, twelve plus; children below this age may still be considered too young to decide for themselves.

When will the courts stop ruling in relation to access?

As a child grows older, the courts will generally be guided more by the wishes of children, as expressed through a court-appointed psychologist's report.

Items that should be included in court orders in relation to access

Problems and resulting frustration can arise because court orders cannot cover every possible eventuality, and no court, except in extreme circumstances, is going to put an order in place which requires its constant supervision. Once an access order is in place, the only recourse to changing it is by going back to court. However, it is my belief that some of the difficulties that arise in relation to access are a result of the fact that court orders are not specific enough for both sides.

While a court will specify when access should take place, it usually will not specify anything else unless specifically asked to do so, and even then there are no guarantees. I list below some of the areas that I believe should be addressed before an access order is put in place, both for the benefit of the parents and of the children.

~ Both parents should have full knowledge of the other parent's residential address and be entitled to know where their children are staying.

~ If taking children to an address for an overnight visit which is not at the residential address, the other parent should be informed. This is not to say that the permission of the custodial parent should be sought, but simply that s/he should be informed of where the children are.

~ Each parent should have a land-line telephone number and/or a mobile number for the other.

~ Each parent should be obliged to keep the other informed of any events that have an impact on continuity of care. By this I mean that, if a young child is, for example, sick and in need of medication during the course of an access visit, the other parent should be informed. A situation should not be allowed to arise where one parent is prescribing medication and the other is not aware of it. There should be total transparency in relation to both the health and care of the children at all times.

Psychologist's report

When a court is determining the access arrangements for a child, it can order, of its own volition or at the request of either party, that a court-appointed child psychologist be called in for the purpose of assisting in determining the correct level of access. Given that it can often be difficult to make a decision when each spouse is arguing his/her own case, usually with opposing views, the court may order that a psychologist's report be sought.

Both parties would then, without their legal representatives and on their own, meet with the psychologist to discuss key aspects of the children's welfare. This is the opportunity for both the parent seeking access and the custodial parent to outline what they are looking for in relation to access. Most people see access as something that just one parent gets, and in a way that is true, but the custodial parent, even if the child is living with him/her, will also want quality time with the children, and this does not necessarily mean dropping them at a crèche or a school and picking them up later.

The psychologist will also meet the children at a visit with each of the parents. If the children are old enough, this may be done at the office of the psychologist or, where relevant, depending on the child's age or other issues, they will visit the child in the homes of both parents to assess how the child is with each. This should not be treated as a competition. It is done to ensure that the level of access awarded is what, in the psychologist's opinion, is in the best interests of the child.

Neither legal team is allowed to inform the court-appointed psychologist of any facts/information without the consent of the other legal team, and such information should never be for the purpose of trying to influence the report in favour of one of the parties. The court will make clear its instruction to the psychologist in its order. The meeting is usually for the purpose of drafting a report to assist the courts, from a professional and impartial point of view by a person who has had time to meet with the parties concerned.

Discussing access can be difficult. However, treat the meeting with the psychologist as an opportunity to express your views without being cross-examined by the other side. At least you will know that time and effort has been expended on assessing the situation and, hopefully, it will be of assistance to the court in making the order.

A psychologist's report is not a free service provided by the courts. It is an additional cost – and sometimes an expensive one. Depending on the circumstances of both parties, the court may order that the costs are divided on a fifty-fifty basis between both parties. If you are lucky, the total cost will be in the hundreds of euro, but you should be aware that it can often stretch into four figures.

WHY THERE ARE NO SET ACCESS ARRANGEMENTS

No two sets of families share the same circumstances. This means that a blanket decision about what is best for the children, according to their age, may be impractical, which is why it is imperative that the courts have discretion in these matters. Some possible variations are as follows:

- ∾ If a child is at home with the custodial parent on a full-time basis, a court may be more generous when allocating time to the parent who is seeking access, as there is a lot of time available.

- ∾ If, however, the child resides with a custodial parent who is working full time, the amount of access awarded to the parent seeking access may be less, as there is less free time available. This would mean that a different access award could be made, at the court's discretion, in order to accommodate the lifestyle of the custodial parent.

- ∾ If one parent works in a job that involves shift work or travel, the time when s/he is available, both mid-week and at weekends, may vary and an order may be varied, at the court's discretion, to accommodate this.

[1 2]

PRE-NUPTIAL AGREEMENTS

We have all read about celebrity weddings, seen the magazine coverage and watched the television clips. A recent celebrity wedding that springs to mind is that of multi-millionaire Paul McCartney and Heather Mills. A lot of the coverage around the wedding highlighted reports that there was no pre-nuptial agreement in place. Many people said this was foolish, others thought it reflected how much he loved his fiancée. Another even more high-profile wedding was that of Catherine Zeta Jones and Michael Douglas. As much as Michael proclaimed his love for Catherine, a highly publicised pre-nuptial agreement was reputed to be a requirement prior to their marriage. While the press were not privy to the details, it was speculated that an amount was agreed in relation to how much Catherine would receive in the event of a divorce – this would be dependent on how long they had been married and how many children they had.

So what is a pre-nuptial agreement (or 'pre-nup', as they are more commonly referred to)? It is a formal, legal agreement made between two people who are about to enter into marriage, outlining in very specific terms what would happen, usually on a financial basis, if their marriage were to end and the parties separate. The items a pre-nup can cover will vary according to their needs and, indeed, according to the assets of the two people concerned. A pre-nup will usually cover such things as property, maintenance, custody and access arrangements in the event that there are any children, and can be specific down to the division of anything, from stocks and shares to the CD collection. It can cover any aspect relating to property or belongings and may even be specific about conditions of the marriage, from the simple to the most bizarre.

While many cynics may say it cannot be true love if one party asks the other to sign a pre-nup, others would argue that, when two people agree to marry, they usually do so at the height of their passion and believing that theirs will be the marriage to end all marriages. When better a time to reach an agreement?

Before I continue, I should make it clear that pre-nuptial agreements have no legal standing in any court of law in Ireland. As such, the current position would appear to be that these contracts are completely unenforceable in this country. So why am I wasting my time talking about them? I suppose it's because of the dreams and aspirations they represent. Two people about to head down the aisle making plans for their future: travelling together, working, maybe even having children together. These dreams are enough to make two people take a vow to commit to each other for the rest of their lives, but unfortunately they have no relevance when it comes to ending that relationship.

However, there is no reason why a couple who have drawn up such an agreement cannot use it in the context of mediation in order to reach their own agreement in relation to a separation. The whole process could be made much quicker, less painful and a great deal less expensive for those who choose to take this route, but only in the context of two people who are willing to enter into separation mediation and move forward based on a written agreement they made when at the height of their love for one another.

Once I would have viewed pre-nups with disdain, but now I view them differently – as something that makes good sense. Given the amount of marriages that fail, and the legal battles and subsequent costs that can ensue, there might well be an argument for having them legally recognised. If two people can, when they no longer feel love for each other, reach a mediated agreement, why can they not be allowed to reach agreement prior to marriage? Prior to divorce in Ireland, pre-nups were seen as a threat to the fabric of the family unit. Given the increasing rate of marital breakdown, the only way a pre-nup damages the fabric of marriage is to make people think a little harder before entering into it – and is that really such a bad thing?

If you do decide to proceed with drawing up a pre-nuptial agreement, you should be aware of a few things:

- Assume that pre-nuptial agreements are not valid and are unenforceable in Ireland.
- If you decide to go ahead and draw one up, make sure that both parties receive separate legal advice.
- While not valid in a court of law, if the marriage ends in separation and both parties are fairly amicable, it could be used by them as a basis for mediation.

The thought of a drawing up a pre-nup at a time when you are planning to spend a lifetime together may seem crazy. However, if you can have the foresight to cater for other potential eventualities in your life – such as illness, unemployment, etc. – surely, while hoping it may never happen, it would make good sense to take out some form of insurance in the event that your marriage does not last. You can hope that you never have to use it, but you may nonetheless be glad of it one day.

[13]

PAPERWORK

No one likes paperwork. It is tiresome, boring and something most people only do when they have to. The legal documents you need to produce are only one part of the paperwork required by a court. Normally there will be a lot of other paperwork, ranging from medical receipts for the children to bank statements, credit card bills, etc., going back several years. Sifting through paperwork is no one's idea of fun, but it is a necessary evil on the separation journey. Here we will look at the various types of paperwork required by the courts. We will do this for two reasons.

~ It will help you to understand what your solicitor is talking about. Any time spent with your solicitor costs money, so, the more prepared you are prior to a meeting, the more value you will get from the meetings. It will also help to make such meetings less stressful and more productive.

~ You are not legally required to have a solicitor or barrister represent you in court. You are entitled to represent yourself (see Chapter 4). If you take this route, you may need to use some of the forms I have shown at the end of this chapter. Blank copies of all these documents are available from the courts. The relevant clerk at the family law court in your area will provide you with a copy.

It is important to read the documents thoroughly, as this will help you understand them.

Even if you are being represented by a solicitor, it is useful to know what the documents they are preparing for you contain and what they look like. Your solicitor is authorised to accept paperwork on your behalf. The only time you should be served directly with any legal documents is if there is an application for an attachment and committal order. This is an order asking for a custodial sentence (imprisonment) to be considered for the respondent. Because of its seriousness, it has to be served on you in person, even if a solicitor is representing you (your solicitor will normally be served with an additional copy). It is not a sinister process at all; a service processor, usually someone who works for your solicitor's firm, will simply call and hand you the paperwork. This ensures that you have had due notice of the order and, if you choose to disregard it, the court will know that you do so of your own volition and not because you did not receive it.

Notice for the fixing of a date for trial

This is a notice for you to attend court, at which time the actual court date will be assigned.

Notice of motion

A notice of motion is the document you will need for interim applications prior to the final hearing of your case. It is also the mechanism to bring the case before the court where it is being dealt with on consent. The applicant, or the applicant's solicitor, will take this document to the court and present it to the court clerk, who will insert the date, time and place of the hearing. You need to provide the original and three copies of this document: one for you, one for the court and one to be served on the respondent. If issuing a motion, you should lodge a grounding affidavit at the same time.

Grounding affidavit

A grounding affidavit is a sworn statement listing your reasons for filing a motion to go to court and the reliefs you are seeking from the court and stating any other relevant facts. If you are filing a notice of motion to go before the court, you accompany it with a grounding affidavit, which is a way of formally presenting both the court and the respondent with the reliefs that are being sought by you from the court.

The Family Law Civil Bill

This is the originating document that you (or your solicitor on your behalf) will be required to fill out when seeking a judicial separation. This constitutes a simple history of your marriage and a description of both parties. It lists the practical information that the court, which has no prior knowledge of you, will need to have.

- Current addresses for both of you.
- Your occupations and your places of employment.
- The date that you got married and the date that you separated.

~ Full details in relation to any children of the marriage.

~ The reasons why the marriage ended and the separation occurred.

~ What reliefs you are looking for (i.e. what financial settlement you are asking the court to make).

Affidavit of service

An affidavit of service is the document that proves that you have indeed served the notice of motion and any other paperwork on the respondent. The document, in order to be relied upon, must be sworn by a practising solicitor or a commissioner for oaths after the relevant paperwork has been served. Essentially, this document records the date on which it was sent and acts as proof of same. Any document served, if not delivered by a service processor, should be sent by registered post and the receipt should be attached to your own copy of the affidavit of service, as proof that the document was indeed sent.

Affidavit of means

See Chapter 9 for a description of the affidavit of means form.

Affidavit of welfare

An affidavit of welfare is the document required if there are any dependent children of the marriage. Once a child is over the age of eighteen and not in full-time education, or up to twenty-three if in full-time education, s/he is no longer considered to be a dependant and this document is no longer required. If, however, your child is a dependant due to, for example, a mental or physical disability and still requires financial assistance from both parents, then you should complete this document. This is the curriculum vitae of your children and is completed in order to help the court assess their needs. If either of you have children from a previous relationship or marriage, details in relation to those children should also be listed. The document will include such things as:

~ The name and age of the children.

~ The address where the children live, who lives with them at that address and who owns the house/apartment/dwelling.

~ If there are others living at the address, their relationship with the children should also be listed (e.g. grandparent, cousin, etc.).

~ The names and addresses of the children's crèches or schools.

~ The cost in relation to those facilities (i.e. crèche or school fees).

~ Whether or not you are in receipt of maintenance for the children.

~ Details of any access arrangements that are in place or a statement as to whether or not the respondent has any contact with the children.

~ Any problematic health issues in relation to either the parents or the children should also be listed and, if necessary, any

details in relation to the medical care that
is provided for that party.

Everyone's circumstances are different, but the affidavit of welfare is designed to give the court a full picture of any children of the marriage. Any details that are not listed above but are highly relevant to the situation must be included.

If the respondent does not dispute any of the facts you have given in the affidavit of welfare, he or she will have no need to complete the schedule in relation to the children.

Timing of documents

There are set procedures and times for both serving and responding to any of the documents outlined here. Once the applicant lodges the documents, the respondent will be given a deadline by which to respond and will then provide their own replying paperwork.

When serving a notice of motion, you must provide the respondent with four clear working days before the case is heard in court.

It you lodge a Family Law Civil Bill for a full hearing, you must provide the respondent with at least ten clear days to enter their appearance. If they fail to do so, you must give another fourteen days before you apply for a motion for judgment.

Adjournments

Each side is free to apply for an adjournment of a hearing, for instance if they feel ill-prepared or require more time to respond. You can either ask the opposing solicitor's side for an adjournment of the date to a later time or can apply to the court on the day for an adjournment. There tends to be more leniency in family law cases, so adjournments are common. It can be very frustrating for the applicant, but, if your solicitor is asked for an adjournment, chances are s/he will agree, as it will probably be granted by the court. If, however, adjournments have already been facilitated prior to the court date, the judge can be asked that no further adjournments be considered. You do not necessarily have to agree to one and can argue against it in court on the day, but there are no guarantees. It all comes down to the discretion of the court. There has to be valid reason for seeking an adjournment. They are most likely to be granted if the required periods of notice for serving and receiving documents have not been complied with.

Record number

In the top right-hand corner of the front page of each of the documents required you will see a space for a record number. This is the number given to your case when it is processed by the court (e.g. 00/1234). The first two digits refer to the year of your initial application and the second set of numbers identifies your case for that particular year. This number is important, as you will need it in all your dealings with the courts. If you require something from the court clerks, you will need to quote this number so they can find your file. All correspondence with the court should also contain this number. It is unique to your case and will not be duplicated for any other case.

Sample paperwork

There now follow some samples of paperwork that may be required for family law proceedings in the circuit court. If you are representing yourself and not using the services of a solicitor, you should contact your local court office and get up-to-date copies of these forms. The samples shown here, however, should help to give you some idea of what to expect.

AN CHÚIRT TEAGHLAIGH CHUARDA
(THE CIRCUIT FAMILY COURT)

RECORD NO.

(*insert circuit court name*) CIRCUIT
COUNTY OF (*insert county name*)

IN THE MATTER OF THE JUDICIAL SEPARATION AND FAMILY LAW REFORM ACT 1989 AND IN THE MATTER OF THE FAMILY LAW ACT 1995

BETWEEN   (*insert name of person making application*)

Applicant

AND

(*insert name of spouse, the person who is responding*)

Respondent

NOTICE FOR THE FIXING OF A DATE FOR TRIAL

TAKE NOTICE, that a date will be fixed for the hearing of the trial of the action on the day of _____ 20___ next at the Circuit Family Court sitting at Court _____ at (insert address of court here)

Dated this _____ day of 20___

Signed: _____
       & Co
       Solicitors

To: The Registrar
       Circuit Court Family Law Office
       (insert address)

To: _____
       & Co
       Solicitors for the Respondent

AN CHÚIRT TEAGHLAIGH CHUARDA
(THE CIRCUIT FAMILY COURT)

RECORD NO.

(*insert circuit court name*) **CIRCUIT**

COUNTY OF (*insert county name*)

IN THE MATTER OF THE JUDICIAL SEPARATION AND FAMILY LAW REFORM ACT 1989 AND IN THE MATTER OF THE FAMILY LAW ACT 1995

BETWEEN (*insert name of person making application*)

Applicant

AND

(*insert name of spouse, the person who is responding*)

Respondent

NOTICE OF MOTION

TAKE NOTICE, that on the ____ day of ____ 20____ at the hour of ____ o'clock or as soon thereafter as it may be heard, application will be made on behalf of the above named Applicant to this Honourable Court sitting at Court ____ for the following relief:

    A.   (*insert reliefs being sought*)

    B   (*insert reliefs being sought*)

AND take notice that the said application will be grounded upon this Notice of Motion and proof of service hereof, the further Affidavit of (***insert name of applicant***), and proof of service thereof, further and other evidence (including oral evidence) as may be adduced by and on behalf of the Applicant, the nature of the case and the reasons to be offered.

Dated the ____ day of ____, 20____.

Signed: _____ Applicant

(*insert name and relevant address here*)

To: The Registrar
        Circuit Court Family Law Office
        (Insert relevant address)

To: (Insert name and address of Respondent's Solicitor)
        (Insert relevant address)

AN CHÚIRT TEAGHLAIGH CHUARDA
(THE CIRCUIT FAMILY COURT)

RECORD NO.

(*insert circuit court name*) CIRCUIT

COUNTY OF (*insert county name*)

IN THE MATTER OF THE JUDICIAL SEPARATION AND FAMILY LAW REFORM ACT 1989 AND IN THE MATTER OF THE FAMILY LAW ACT 1995

BETWEEN   (*insert name of person making application*)

Applicant

AND

(*insert name of spouse, the person who is responding*)

Respondent

AFFIDAVIT OF THE APPLICANT

I, (*insert name*) of (*insert address*), aged 18 years and upwards to here **MAKE OATH** and **SAY** as follows:

1.   I am the Applicant in the above entitled proceedings and I make this Affidavit from facts within my own knowledge save where otherwise appears and where so appearing I believe the same to be true.

2.   *(All further points will be listing the reliefs you are looking for and the reasons for same and any other relevant material facts – each point should be numbered separately)*

> **SWORN** by the said (*insert name*) this
> ____ day of ____ 20__ at ____ in the
> county of the city of ____ before me a
> Commissioner for Oaths/Practising
> Solicitor and I know the deponent

_____

COMMISSIONER FOR OATHS/PRACTISING SOLICITOR

AN CHÚIRT TEAGHLAIGH CHUARDA
(THE CIRCUIT FAMILY COURT)

RECORD NO.

(*insert circuit court name*) **CIRCUIT**
COUNTY OF (*insert county name*)

IN THE MATTER OF THE JUDICIAL SEPARATION AND FAMILY LAW REFORM ACT 1989 AND IN THE MATTER OF THE FAMILY LAW ACT 1995

BETWEEN   (*insert name of person making application*)

Applicant

AND

(*insert name of spouse, the person who is responding*)

Respondent

FAMILY LAW CIVIL BILL

You are hereby required within 10 days after the service of this Civil Bill upon you, to enter, or cause to be entered with the County Registrar, or his or her office at (*insert the address of your local family court here*) an appearance to answer the Claim of (*insert the applicant's name and address here*), the Applicant herein as endorsed hereon.

AND TAKE NOTICE THAT unless you do enter an appearance, you will be held to have admitted the said claim and the Applicant may proceed therein and judgment may be given against you in your absence without further notice.

AND FURTHER TAKE NOTICE THAT if you intend to defend the proceedings on any grounds, you must not only enter an Appearance as aforesaid, but also within ten 10 days after your Appearance deliver a statement in writing showing the nature and grounds of your Defence.

The Appearance and Defence may be entered by posting same to the said Office and by giving copies to the Applicant and/or his/her Solicitor by post.

Dated the (*Date*) day of (*Month*) 20___

Signed: (*Signature of the Applicant*)

———————————————

(*Typed name of Applicant*)
APPLICANT

To: (*Name of Respondent*)
    (*Address of Respondent*)

ENDORSEMENT OF CLAIM

1. The Applicant and Respondent were married on the (*insert date*) at (*insert details of place of marriage*).
2. The Applicant and Respondent have been living apart for (*insert number*) years, since (*insert date*).
3. During that time the Applicant lived at (*insert full address*). The Respondent lived at (*insert full address*).
4. Occupations of both parties.
5. There was an issue of the marriage, namely: (*list children's names and their dates of birth here*) or there are no children of the marriage.
6. Details of present and past family homes.
7. Description of any land or premises referred to in the Civil Bill, and whether it is registered or unregistered land.

AND THE APPLICANT CLAIMS:

(*Here provide a numbered list of the individual reliefs sought, by reference to sections of the Act*)

AND FURTHER TAKE NOTICE that, in any cases where financial relief is sought by either party, you must file with the Defence herein, or in any event within 20 days after the service of this Civil Bill upon you, at the aforementioned Circuit Court Office an Affidavit of Means (and, where appropriate, an Affidavit of Welfare) in the manner prescribed by the Rules of this Court, and serve a copy of same as provided by the Rules of this Court on the Applicant or his Solicitor at the address provided below.

Dated the _____ day of _____ 20____

Signed: _____
        Applicant

To: The Registrar,
Circuit Family Court
and/

To: Respondent's solicitor

AN CHÚIRT TEAGHLAIGH CHUARDA
(THE CIRCUIT FAMILY COURT)

RECORD NO.

(*insert circuit court name*) CIRCUIT
COUNTY OF (*insert county name*)

IN THE MATTER OF THE JUDICIAL SEPARATION AND FAMILY LAW REFORM ACT 1989 AND IN THE MATTER OF THE FAMILY LAW ACT 1995

BETWEEN (*insert name of person making application*)

Applicant

AND

(*insert name of spouse, the person who is responding*)

Respondent

AFFIDAVIT OF SERVICE

I, (*insert name*) of (*insert address*), aged 18 years and upwards MAKE OATH and say as follows:

1. That on the _____ day of _____ 20___, I did serve on the Respondent of (*insert address here*) a true copy of Notice of Motion dated the (*insert date here*) upon which I endorsed my name, by Personal Service/Registered Post. [delete as appropriate]

2. I beg to refer to the certificate of posting (*or insert name of relevant proof of delivery*) of the said envelope attached hereto and signed by me prior to the swearing hereof.

3. I say that the envelope has not been returned undelivered.

4. I make this Affidavit from facts within my own knowledge save where otherwise appear and where so appearing I believe the same to be true.

SWORN by

This (*day*) day of (*month*) 20____

Before me a practising Solicitor and
I know the Deponent/Declarant

_____   _____

Deponent/Declarant   **Practising Solicitor**

FORM NO. 1

AN CHÚIRT TEAGHLAIGH CHUARDA
(THE CIRCUIT FAMILY COURT)

RECORD NO.

(*insert circuit court name*) CIRCUIT

COUNTY OF (*insert county name*)

IN THE MATTER OF THE JUDICIAL SEPARATION AND FAMILY LAW REFORM ACT 1989 AND IN THE MATTER OF THE FAMILY LAW ACT 1995

BETWEEN   (*insert name of person making application*)

Applicant

AND

(*insert name of spouse, the person who is responding*)

Respondent

AFFIDAVIT OF WELFARE

I, (*insert your name, address and occupation*), aged 18 years and upwards, MAKE OATH and say as follows:

1. I say that I am the Applicant in the above proceedings and I make this Affidavit of Welfare from facts within my own knowledge, save where otherwise appears, and where so appearing, I believe the same to be true.
2. I say and believe that the facts set out in the Schedule hereto are true.

SCHEDULE
Part I – Details of children

1. Details of the children born to (or adopted by) the Respondent and Applicant.

Forenames	Surnames	Dates of birth

2. Details of other children of the family, or children to whom either of the parties is in loco parentis. (*name any children that you may have from a previous or current relationship*)

Forenames   Surnames   Dates of birth

_____   _____   _____

Part II – Arrangements for children of the family

3. Home details (*insert your current residential address*)

    (a) The address at which the children now live.
    (b) Details of the number of living rooms, bedrooms at the above address(es).
    (c) Is the house rented or owned? Name the tenant(s) or owner(s).
    (d) Is the rent or mortgage being paid regularly and by whom?
    (e) Give the names of all other person living with the children, full-time or part-time, and state their relationship to the children.
    (f) Will there be any changes to these arrangements? If so, give details.

Part III – Education and training

    (a) Give details of the school, college or place of training attended by each child.
    (b) Do the children have special educational needs? If so, please specify.
    (c) Is the school, college or place of training fee-paying? If so, how much are the fees per term/year? Are fees being paid regularly and, if so, by whom?
    (d) Will there be any changes in these circumstances? If so, give details.

Part IV – Childcare

(a) Which parent looks after the children from day to day?
     If responsibility is shared, give details.
(b) Give details of work commitments of both parents.
(c) Does someone look after the children when the parents
     are not there? If yes, give details.
(d) Who looks after the children during school holidays?
(e) Will there be any changes to these arrangements? If so,
     give details.

Part V – Maintenance

(a) Does the Respondent pay towards the upkeep of the
     children? If so, give details. Specify any other sources of
     maintenance.
(b) Is the maintenance referred to above paid under Court
     order? If so, give details.
(c) Has maintenance been agreed for the children? If so,
     give details.
(d) If not, will you be applying for a maintenance order
     from the Court?

Part VI – Contact with the children

(a) Do the children see the Respondent? Give details.
(b) Do the children stay overnight and/or have holiday
     visits with the Respondent? Give details.
(c) Will there be any changes to these arrangements? If so,
     give details.

Part VII – Health

(a) Are the children generally in good health? Give details
     of any serious disability or chronic illness suffered by
     any of the children.
(b) Do any of the children have any special health needs?
     Give details of care needed and how it is to be provided.
(c) Are the Applicant or Respondent generally in good
     health? If not, give details.

Part VIII – Care and other Court proceedings

(a) Are any of the children in the care of a health board or under the supervision of a social worker or probation officer? If so, give details.

(b) Have there been any Court proceedings involving any of the children? If so, give details. (All relevant Court orders should be annexed.)

> Sworn by the said (name) before me, a practising solicitor/Commissioner for Oaths, on (date),
>
> at _____ and I know the deponent.
>
> Signed: (name) _____

Filed this _____ day of _____ 20__
by (*name and address*) solicitors for the Applicant.

To:
The Registrar,
Circuit Family Court
And/

Solicitor for the Respondent

[1 4]

LOOKING
AHEAD

My journey through judicial separation and, eventually, divorce, was long and difficult and the emotions I experienced over the process ranged from despair and isolation to joy, relief and happiness. One of the most important lessons I have learned – and something which in fact I believe I needed to learn – is that, if your past colours your future in a way that prevents you from leaving yourself open to pleasurable things, then your past indeed has won and your future will be bleak.

Even though my marriage ended and I found the ensuing separation difficult, for a whole host of reasons, I still believe that marriage to the right person is a very positive thing. To the wrong person, it can be a living nightmare. Many people feel that separation is their worst nightmare. However, with the benefit of hindsight you may come to see that, in fact, it was the process of waking from one. I know it was for me.

I do not believe that time heals all wounds, but it does give us the distance to look back on difficult periods in our lives with a degree of objectivity. We can learn from past mistakes and come to understand why they happened, but ultimately we need to leave the pain behind and move on.

When asked if I have regrets, my answer is no. We move on, albeit slowly sometimes, but, when I look back on my journey and see where I am now, I know that I have indeed travelled a long way. One of the most poignant moments for me in the whole process was when, on the day I got my divorce, one of the people closest to me told me they were happier for me on the day I got divorced than they were on my wedding day. This was a simple and honest acknowledgement that the decision I made to get divorced was better than the one that brought me there – and that the happiness I was so clearly feeling was a pleasure for them to see. As they say, it's a strange road that has no turning.

Is there life after separation? Yes. Is there love after separation? Yes. All things are indeed possible.

When I found myself in the position of being separated and on my own, I thought it was the worst thing in the world. I was hurt, shocked and angry all at the same time. I was scared too. Not only was I separated, but I was also pregnant, with a new home and a new job. It was a lot of change to deal with all at the same time, but it's a better road that I am on now and a far happier and more rewarding one.

With the passage of time, I have come to know myself and what I am capable of – and that has been the best journey of all. The things I once grieved for are no longer relevant; they belong to a past that seems like a dream. I give thanks for my separation, as the quality of life and happiness I now experience are greater than I have ever known before. It was well worth the journey. One day I may marry again, and, then again, I may not – but neither possibility holds any fear for me.

One thing we all have is the ability to choose. It may sound corny, but, although we may not be able to change the path we are on, we can change the attitude that we face it with – and this in itself can make the journey less painful. However, learning how to do this takes time. The important thing is to learn to keep looking forward. If we keep looking back, we may never see what is ahead – and we could be missing a hell of a view and a lot of possibilities. While it is good to carry with us the lessons we have learned, it is not so good to carry some of the baggage we pick up along the way.

Parts of this book may seem like a cautionary tale. What you need to take from it will vary according to your own specific circumstances. The best advice I can give is to think carefully about whether you really want, and actually need, to travel this road. Going to court is a serious step, and, like marriage, one which should not be taken lightly. Make sure you have no other option left open to you. Is your marriage really over? Could you work things out if you really put your mind to it? If you feel you have no other option, do everything you can to reach your own outcome as two individuals, without having to go to court.

In the course of my journey, I have heard many sad stories from people who feel that the system has not served them well. I have also heard many hardship stories, from both sides – whether it be an estranged spouse struggling to pay maintenance or a single parent struggling to raise a family without financial support from the other spouse. The court system tries to find a solution that works for the children and for the parents, but this inevitably requires compromise.

While many people are dissatisfied with the court process, in its favour I have to say that it does at least provide a starting-point. It tries to make both parties accountable and, in its own way, attempts to bring an adversarial situation to an end and find an appropriate solution for all parties. While it is the last port of call, it is at least a means to an end.

May your journey be short and your recovery swift, and may you arrive at your destination with some hope of building a foundation for a new and brighter future.

LEGAL AID FORMS

LEGAL AID BOARD

APPLICATION FOR LEGAL SERVICES

The Law Centre will assist you in completing this form

1. **Name:** _____

    Address: _____

    _____

    _____

    Telephone No: _____

2. **Subject Matter:** (a) Family Law ❏ (b) Non Family ❏* [*Tick as appropriate*

    Please specify: _____

    _____

    _____

***NOTE:** If there is more than one matter, you must use separate application forms.

YOU SHOULD READ THE FOLLOWING DECLARATION CAREFULLY BEFORE YOU SIGN BELOW

(i)   I have received the Note for the Information of the Applicant

(ii) I apply for legal aid or advice or both for the matter(s) indicated at *2 above*

(iii) I understand that legal advice and legal aid are separate matters and that I may onl
      require legal advice

(iv) Should I require legal aid, I understand that my application will only be considere
      by the Board after I have received legal advice and/or when I have instructed m
      solicitor to submit it for consideration

SIGNED: (Applicant) _____ Date: _____

EGAL AID BOARD FORM 1   STATEMENT OF MEANS

Name:

Address:

Phone: PPS NO:

You should read the following DECLARATION carefully before you sign this Form. If you do not understand any part of the form or the declaration please contact the Law Centre.

- I confirm that to the best of my knowledge the information which I have given is correct.
- I understand that the furnishing of incorrect information or the failure to disclose any material fact may lead to the withdrawal of legal advice and/or aid in which event I may be liable for costs incurred.
- I understand that if my means change I must inform the Board.
- I confirm that the value of disposable capital assets of any kind whatsoever which I possess does not exceed €320,000.
- I understand that the contribution which I shall be required to pay will not be determined finally by the Board until my means have been verified.
- The Board may request the Department of Social, Community and Family Affairs [or another State body] to investigate the means of any person applying for, or in receipt of, legal services including random spot checks.

SIGNED: Date:

Note: Should you wish to make an application for legal aid you will have to complete a Statement of Means – FORM 2 in relation to your capital resources. You need not complete this Form however if your capital resources are such that you can sign the certificate below.

CERTIFICATE

I certify that the value of capital assets which I possess does not exceed €3,200 and/or that the value of my interest, if any, in the family home does not exceed €190,500

SIGNED: Date:

INCOME

Please complete columns A or B, whichever you find most convenient. If your spouse/partner is the opposing party it is not necessary to provide information on his/her resources. Income as declared should be supported by documentary evidence, e.g. social welfare book, recent pay slip, bank statements, up-to-date accounts etc.

TYPE OF INCOME		(A) € PER WEEK		(B) € PER MONTH	
		SELF	SPOUSE/ PARTNER	SELF	SPOUSE/ PARTNER
1	EMPLOYMENT				
2	SOCIAL WELFARE/ HEALTH ACTS				
	State Type				
3	MAINTENANCE RECEIVED				
4	BUSINESS/ OTHER OCCUPATION				
5	OTHER SOURCE (e.g. a FÁS Course, Pensions, etc.)				
6	BENEFIT IN KIND (e.g. a car, accommodation, insurance premiums, etc.)				

DEDUCTIONS

ease complete columns A or B, whichever you find most convenient. The figures quoted
ust be actual amounts paid and should be supported by relevant receipts etc.

YPE OF INCOME	(A) € PER WEEK		(B) € PER MONTH	
	SELF	SPOUSE/ PARTNER	SELF	SPOUSE/ PARTNER
ACCOMMODATION				
INCOME TAX				
PRSI				
CHILD CARE (working parent)				
MAINTENANCE PAYMENTS				
AGES OF DEPENDENT CHILDREN:				
OTHER DEPENDANTS (specify)				

LEGAL AID BOARD FORM 2   STATEMENT OF CAPITA

Name:	
Address:	

Phone:		PPS NO:	

1.   MONEY – EURO AMOUNT

	Self €	Spouse/Partner €
On Hands		
Bank Accounts		
An Post Account		
Building Society		
Credit Union		
Other Institution		

FAMILY HOME (If owned by you or your spouse/partner)

	Self €	Spouse/Partner €
Family Home Address		
Mortgagee		
Outstanding Mortgagee		
Monthly Repayments		
Outstanding Mortgage		
Value of Home		
Value of Contents		

LAND

	Self €	Spouse/Partner €
Market Value of Land		
Acreage		
Do you farm the land?		
Monthly Repayments		
Outstanding Charge/Mortgage		

4. PROPERTY OTHER THAN LAND OR FAMILY HOME (including farm buildings)

	Self €	Spouse/Partner €
Type of Property		
Euro Value		
Mortgagee		
Outstanding Mortgage		
Monthly Repayments		

5. STOCKS, SHARE, OTHER SECURITIES – Euro Value

Type of Stock, Share of Security	Self €	Spouse/Partner €
A.		
B.		

6. INTEREST IN A COMPANY, BUSINESS OR PROPERTY-OWNING BODY – Euro Value

Name of Company, Business or Body	Self €	Spouse/Partner €
A.		
B.		

7. LIFE INSURANCE OR ENDOWMENT POLICIES – Euro Value

Type of Policy	Self €	Spouse/Partner €
A.		
B.		

8. DEBTS OWED TO THE APPLICANT – Euro Value

Owed by Whom	Self €	Spouse/Partner €
A.		
B.		

9. VALUABLES (Other than personal items of jewellery – Euro Value)

Nature of Valuable	Self €	Spouse/Partner €
A.		
B.		

10. OTHER CAPITAL RESOURCES (e.g. Car) – Euro Value

Nature of Resource	Self €	Spouse/Partner €
.		
.		

11. CAPITAL PAYMENTS ON FOOT OF LOAN (not shown at 2, 3 & 4 above)

Loan Advanced By:	Loan Advanced To:	Loan Obtained For:	Outstanding Balance €	Monthly Capital Payment €
A.				
B.				

11. LEGALLY ENFORCEABLE DEBTS

Creditor:	Nature of Debt:	Amount Payable €
A.		
B.		

▼ DECLARATION

You should read this declaration carefully before you sign the Form. If you do not understand any part of the form or the declaration please contact the Law Centre.

> ➢ I hereby declare that to the best of my knowledge the information which I have given is correct
> ➢ I understand that the furnishing of incorrect information or the failure to disclose any material fact may lead to the withdrawal of legal advice and/or aid in which event I may be liable for costs incurred
> ➢ I understand that if my means change I must inform the Board

SIGNED: _____

DATE: _____

INDEX

access rights, 9, 10, 11, 22,
  66, 92, 93, 105, 106,
  134, 146, 147–54, 163
  access orders, 86, 147–52
accommodation, 1
adjournment *see* courts
adultery, 8
affidavit of means, 114–30,
  162
affidavit of service, 162
  sample form, 174–5
affidavit of welfare, 162–4
  sample form, 176–9
annulment, 4–5
assets and property, 17, 20,
  22, 92, 99–100, 101–2,
  115, 118, 130, 144–5
  see also pre-nuptial
    agreements
attachment and committal
  order, 160

Bar Council of Ireland, 30,
  33, 76, 77
barring and safety orders, 92,
  106–7, 112
barristers, 13, 24, 30–43,
  44–5, 78, 82–3, 84, 85,
  96
  'devils', 41, 45
  pre-hearing consultation,
    34
  professional fees, 23, 39,
    41–2

settlement meetings, 40,
  87–8
birthing costs *see* children

children, 1, 3, 66, 134, 138,
  150–1, 163–4
  birthing costs, 92, 105–6
  and court hearings, 75,
    138
  crèche costs, 25, 163
  and the family home,
    96–7, 137
  health considerations
    (disabilites) of, 163–4
  passports for, 92, 105
  and succession rights, 5,
    101–2
  see also access rights;
    custody and
    guardianship;
    maintenance;
    psychologist's reports
Civil Legal Aid Act (1995), 60
Civil Liability and Courts Bill
  (2004), 73–4, 76–8
costs, ix, 17, 22–3, 60,
  108–9, 111–12, 142,
  145, 154
  order for, 35
  see also legal aid
court orders, 51, 82, 88–9,
  90, 91–2, 109, 134,
  139–41, 147, 151–4,
  160–1

court orders (*cont.*)
  amending in cases of error,
    109–10
  appealing, 110, 142
  breach of an order, 111,
    134, 139–42
  see also costs; specific
    orders; maintenance;
    access rights
courts, 2, 21, 32, 44–5,
    73–89, 90–107,
    108–113, 137–9, 156
  abroad, 143
  adjournment, 41, 47, 50,
    81, 164–5
  administration staff, 74,
    78, 112
  adversarial separation, 15,
    29
  appeals, 2, 110–11, 142
  circuit court, 31, 46, 89,
    111, 112, 138,
    141–2, 166
  district court, 46, 112,
    137–8, 141
  family court processes,
    36–7, 48, 50, 54, 56,
    58, 73, 78–87, 88–9
  high court, 46, 111
  lodging paperwork, 47,
    159–60
  magistrate's court (UK),
    143
  notice for the fixing of a
    date for trial, 160
  sample form, 167
  opening times, 85–6
  'specially fixed date', 81
  see also court orders; in-
    camera rule;
    paperwork
custody and guardianship, 22,
    66, 92, 93–4, 134

debts and liabilities, 118, 121,
    127
Department of Social,
    Community and Family
    Affairs, 132, 133
desertion, 8
divorce, 9–11
  grounds for, xi, 11
  uncontested, 9–10
divorce referendum, x
domestic violence, 8–9, 77
  see also barring and safety
    orders

endorcement of claim, 173
Enforcement of Court Orders
    Act (1940), 141

family home, 3, 22, 25, 49,
    94–9, 144–5
  and annulment, 5
  ownership and occupation
    of, 92, 95, 96–9
  sale of, 98–9
  see also assets and property
family law, 75–8, 79, 140,
    166
Family Law Civil Bill, 161–2,
    164
  sample form, 171–2
finances, 114–33
  financial statements, 122,
    123
  tax liability, 132

see also affidavit of means
financial orders, 21

garnishee order, 140–1
grounding affidavit, 35, 51,
    161
grounds for separation, 7–9,
    162

Heads of Agreement, 6, 21

in-camera rule, 28, 73–4,
    75–8
interim maintenance order,
    143

Law Society, 28, 76, 77
lay litigant representation,
    44–59, 145, 159
  changing to legal
      representation, 49–50
  correspondence, 58–9, 166
  in court, 55–7
  preparing for the court
      case, 53–5
  taking legal advice for, 52,
      58
legal aid, 60–72
  assessment time, 66
  costs, 62, 67
  forms, 62–4, 184–92
  legal advice, 61–3
  Legal Aid Board centres,
      68–72
  Legal Aid Certificate, 66,
      67
  means test, 61, 63, 65
  qualifications for, 62

maintenance, 3, 5, 10, 11,
    22, 25, 35, 49, 86, 92,
    112, 129, 130, 131,
    132–3, 134–46, 163
  alternatives to, 144–5
  appeal of an order for, 142
  arrears, 141–2, 145
  breach of maintenance
      payments, 140
  from spouse living abroad,
      143
  lump sum payments, 22,
      92, 103–4, 145
  spousal maintenance,
      137–8
  variance of maintenance
      order, 140, 142
  see also garnishee order,
      interim maintenance
      order
mediated agreements, 5–7,
    15, 21, 66, 149, 157
  see also pre-nuptial
      agreements
Money Advice Budgeting
    Service (MABS), 133
motion of judgment, 164

'no fault' policy, 8
notice of motion, 51, 160–1,
    162, 164
  sample form, 168–9

paperwork, 47, 49, 51, 58,
    62, 86, 159–79
  errors in, 112
  financial statements, 122,
      123
  legal aid forms, 62–4

paperwork (*cont.*)
  lodging, 47
  record number, 165
  serving and receiving, 47,
    48, 51, 164, 165
  samples of, 167–79
  see also specific orders
parental guardianship, 5
passports *see* children
pension adjustment order,
  100–1
pension rights, 22, 92,
  100–1, 115
pre-nuptial agreements,
  155–8
property *see* assets and
    property; family home
property adjustment order, 96
protection order, 106
psychologist's reports, 150,
  151, 152–4

record number *see* paperwork
reliefs *see* court orders
remarriage, 4–5, 9, 97
replying affidavit, 51
representing yourself *see* lay
  litigant representation

separation agreements, 3–4,
  6, 9, 95, 156–8
  and divorce, 10
  see also mediated
    agreements, pre-
    nuptial agreements

service of motion, 51
settlement meetings, 40, 87–8
social welfare, 132–3, 139
solicitors, 3–4, 12–29, 78, 85,
  96
  advice on mediation, 6–7,
    21, 149, 157
  changing, 26–8
  and court order, 89
  initial consultation, 16–17,
    18–20, 21, 27
  Legal Aid Board panel, 66
  professional fees, 22–4, 27,
    42
  representing clients in
    court, 46
  terms of reference, 24, 42
  working with barristers,
    30, 31, 32, 33–5, 39,
    40
statement of means form,
  63–4
statement of means (capital)
  form, 64
succession rights, 5, 22, 92,
  101–2
sworn affidavit, 82
  sample form, 170

violence *see* domestic violence

wills, 102